Creative Crafts
with Wool and Flax

MOLLY DUNCAN'S *Spin Your Own Wool* (1968) was a landmark in the literature of craftwork in Australia and New Zealand. Composed by this gifted practitioner and teacher, its simple and lucid directions, assisted by clear photographs and line drawings, gave it a practical value that has never been excelled.

Creative Crafts with Wool and Flax, the natural sequel to *Spin Your Own Wool*, carries the craftworker forward from the first processes of spinning, dyeing and simple weaving to their applications in knitting, advanced weaving, rugmaking and embroidery with the same clear and helpful guidance that distinguished the author's first book.

An added dimension is given by the inclusion of flax work; the relative virtues and practical blending of home-spun and commercial threads are fully explained; and a special feature running through the book is the importance of colour and texture, and how startlingly beautiful effects may be obtained from their use.

CREATIVE CRAFTS
WITH
WOOL AND FLAX

MOLLY DUNCAN

Photographs by George Bull

Line drawings by Julius Petro

a Bell Handbook

G. BELL AND SONS LTD,
LONDON

First New Zealand Edition 1971
published by A.H. & A.W. Reed Ltd

First British Edition 1973
published by G. Bell and Sons Ltd,
York House, Portugal Street,
London, W.C.2.

ISBN 0 7135 1739 5

Typesetting by New Zealand Typesetters Ltd, Wellington
Printed by Dai Nippon Printing Co. (International) Ltd, Hong Kong

Contents

Acknowledgments

I EXTEND MY THANKS to all who have helped with the publication of this book, especially to the photographer, Mr George Bull; to our friends who have made available their own handiwork, including Mrs McPhail of Waipaoa; Miss Heather Mill of Wellington; Mrs Alice McFarlane of the Wellington Embroiderers' Guild; and to Mrs Joan Walmsley, a member of the London Embroiderers' Guild, organiser of the Cathedral Church Kneeler Projects of the Wellington Diocese, and designer of several hundred kneelers. To Mrs Oriel Hoskin, a textile designer, and Mr Colin Gardner, a wool expert, my sincere gratitude for their practical advice and assistance.

    My thanks, too, to my publishers for their confidence in me and their expert help in the preparation of this sequel to *Spin Your Own Wool*.

Wellington, 1970.   M.D.

Introduction

I WROTE *Spin Your Own Wool* primarily to teach the technique of making a thread on a spinning wheel. To the many spinners who have mastered this technique, a new world of created threads has unfolded and the spinning wheel itself has become a very versatile piece of equipment. The hand-spinner realises now that he can design a cloth, no matter whether it be knitted, crocheted or woven, by ornamenting the yarn during spinning. In short, these textural effects give the personal difference to the handmade garment that distinguishes it from the mass-produced machine product. To justify the extra hours devoted to the making of a personal product the hand-spinner must avoid imitating the machine yarns but he should use them to enhance his own individual product—the differing techniques intermarry well.

Hence *Creative Crafts with Wool and Flax* is planned as a pattern book—as a stimulus to the creative ability inherent in all home-spinners who wish to explore the potential of our natural fibres—so plentiful and so readily accessible to town and country folk alike, and so much the envy of craftsmen in other parts of the world.

Creating with threads is an age-old craft and, therefore, there is very little that is virtually new to discover; but spinning and weaving are very much alive today because the artist-craftsman's skill and vision have departed from tradition and found new means of expression with both natural and synthetic fibres. Where natural fibres flourish more plentifully in one country than in another, so the local craftsman develops more skill and imagination in that medium—the Maoris of New Zealand with their flax *Phormium tenax*, the American Indians with their baskets of yucca, willow and horsehair, the Africans with cotton, the Irish with their linen—to mention but a few.

Readers who wish to follow up the study of traditional Maori uses of *Phormium tenax* will find special interest and inspiration in *The Art of Taaniko Weaving*, by S. M. Mead, published by A. H. & A. W. Reed Ltd.

With the hope that the artist-craftsmen of Australia and New Zealand will bring new concepts to their natural local fibres, I selected the title *Creative Crafts with Wool and Flax* and sincerely hope my readers will take up the challenge and be inspired to find new ways of expression within the inherent potential of these fibres.

An abstract panel inspired by a garden was designed, hand-woven and embroidered by Joan Walmsley: an example of needlework and pulled fabric work on a fine hand-woven linen background.

    Materials used: Handspun wool, fleece wool, linen and cotton threads.

    Stitches used: Spider web, long-leg cross stitch, satin stitch, back stitch, couching, fancy hemstitch, etc.

Chapter 1

PLANNING OUR THREADS

COLOUR, design, and texture combine to make a fabric, and throughout this book the word *texture* will occur time and again. But what do we mean by it? Any interlacing of threads, from the finest-woven soft silks in plain tabby weave to the coarsest twine weaving, holding together raised pieces of tree bark, seaweeds, shells, beads, etc.—all these show *texture*. It is a word that has changed in meaning from its original Latin *texere* to weave; its new interpretation denotes "rough texture", an almost three-dimensional description of the surface. Working with yarns, spinning and dyeing them, selecting and blending commercial threads, planning and forming the design—these all build surface texture, and the field of experimentation is enormous.

To avoid any disappointment in our designing there are a few principles to consider. A surface pattern made with elaborate yarns requires a simple weave. In contrast, a much-patterned "Whig Rose" or "Fox's Chase" in overshot weave loses its balanced geometric appearance unless an even regular yarn is used for its construction.

It is important to plan the quality of the fabric for the purpose for which it is intended: a furnishing fabric that has to drape well in folds or pleats cannot be woven in a stiff yarn; an upholstery fabric must be of a firm weave with no long floating threads to catch and pull apart; table mats must lie flat on the table with no protruding clumps of threads that may cause plates to be unsteady.

Make the most of what science offers us today for new textures and new colours—man-made fibres deserve more study by hand-spinners to add more life and sparkle to an otherwise second-grade fleece. Not every sheep can grow the right quality staple length and the exact coloration that spinners require for a particular purpose.

It is true that raw materials such as our flax and wool are full of suggestions to the craftsman—the more he works them with his hands, understanding the materials' resistance, their potency, their weakness, their charm, their dullness—the more stimulating ideas for textile variations will unfold in his mind. Our ancestors in their search for clothing for warmth, for containers to hold foodstuffs, and for personal adornment could be an inspiration to modern textile designers, in the way they understood and handled the raw materials and made them both meaningful and beautiful.

TAKING A BETTER LOOK AT OUR HOMESPUN WOOL

There is controversy about the qualities of a good or a bad homespun wool yarn. So much depends on the purpose for which the spinner plans to use his yarn and his wisdom in selecting the right wool for the right job. Even the terms homespun or handspun are being used to mean the same thing although a slight differentiation between the two is becoming common. Handspun is self explanatory—a thread spun by hand, whether it be done on a spinning wheel or any of the numerous types of hand spindles. The word homespun is being used as a description of the yarn itself, just as the terms loop yarn, flake yarn, etc., denote the appearance.

The use of the spun yarn should be considered in assessing good and bad spinning. However, there are certain qualities for evaluating homespun yarn for knitting, crochet and weaving, whether it be single ply, fine 2-ply or thick ply for a real "bulkie". Top priority in judging should be *softness*—the feel of the yarn to the touch and the feel of the finished cloth. There are plenty of opportunities to use harsh wools in rugmaking and in certain upholstery materials.

The virtues of a good soft yarn will depend, firstly, on the *quality* of the wool (and the word quality in wool-terms refers to its fineness); and, secondly, on the amount of twist during spinning. Give only just sufficient twist to ensure strength in the thread.

A harsh wool knitted into a polo-neck sweater is too coarse and uncomfortable around the neck, and is certainly an irritant for a small child's tender skin. Australia and New Zealand produce the finest wools in the world, so why shouldn't the craftsmen of these countries learn to select the best their country can offer them?

The hair-like fibre in wool is called *kemp* and is not difficult to recognise. It is harsh to touch and has no crimp, and in colour looks chalky-white. Kemp in wool reflects the light and will not dye the same colour

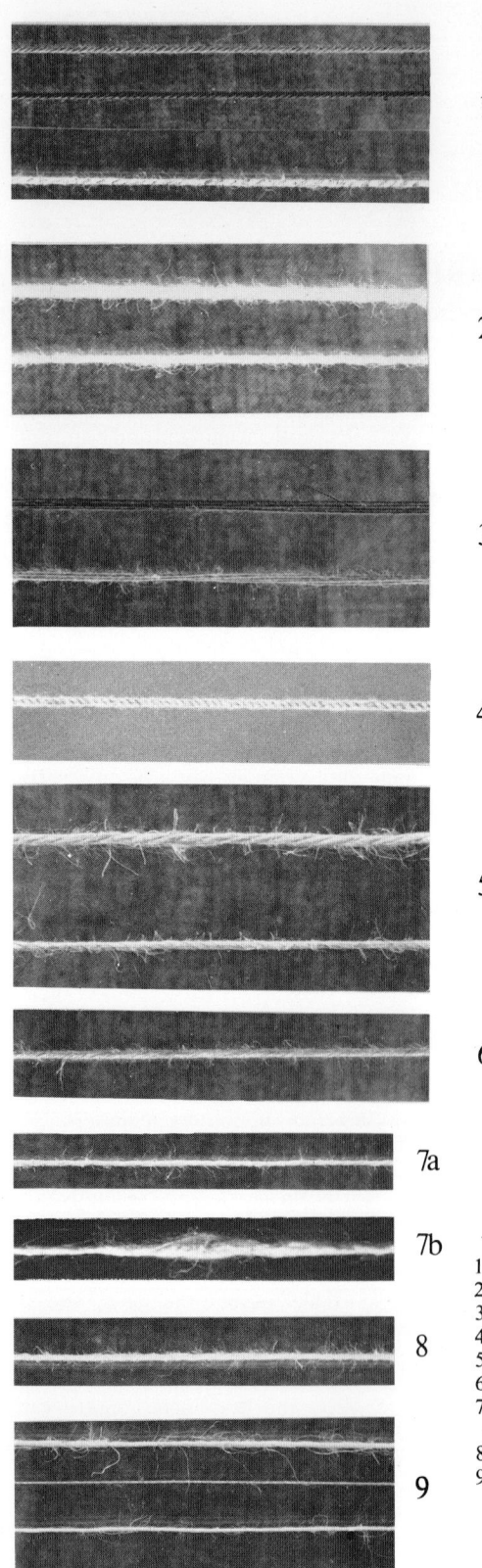

1

2

3

4

5

6

7a

7b

8

9

shade as pure wool. Sometimes this is an advantage as in Harris or other heavy tweeds where the kemp forms a surface texture.

Second priority in judging a homespun yarn would be a *consistent yarn size*, which is achieved by developing a regularity of rhythm in both hand and foot movements during spinning. Some irregularities will occur, and should be there, to give the thread the distinctive homespun look; but these irregularities can still be consistent within the given yarn size.

This same consistency applies to plying, whether it be 2-, 3- or 4-ply—the threads will twist evenly if the rhythm of the hand and foot is regular.

In planning our threads it is often effective to ply homespun yarn with commercial yarns so as to accent colour or texture, or just to add strength.

COMMERCIAL THREADS

The amount of twist in commercial yarn is an important factor in the thread to be made and in the cloth that is to be produced. It determines the appearance as well as the durability and serviceability of the cloth. Fine yarns require more twist than coarse yarns. Warp yarns are given more twist than weft yarns, and commercially-produced yarns are treated with heat and steam to prevent the yarn from untwisting or kinking. This can be applied by steam-ironing the yarn in hank form.

Yarns intended for soft-surface cloth are given only a slight twist. Yarns intended for smooth-surface cloth are given much more twist. This gives the cloth more strength, smoothness, elasticity, and some wrinkle resistance.

Yarn may be twisted in two ways, S or Z, and this can be determined by observing the yarn carefully by unwinding a little of the thread and untwisting it. Crepe effects are produced by using both S and Z yarns alternately in the warp and weft.

YARN COUNTS: In the spinning process there is a fixed relation between the weight of the original quantity of fibre and the length of the yarn produced. This relation indicates the thickness of the yarn. It is determined by the extent the yarn is drawn out, and it is designated by numbers which are called the *yarn count*. The standard for the yarn count in cotton is 1 pound of

1. GIMPS: Three examples, same size (showing hard twist).
2. COTTONS: Two examples, same size (showing soft twist).
3. MILL COTTON: Two examples—fine strands grouped but not twisted.
4. ENSIGN LACING: Tight hard twist.
5. LINEN FLAX SEAMING TWINE: Two examples (strong clear stripped fibre).
6. LINEN LOCKSTITCH: Size 2/7 cord S twist with a shiny finish.
7(a). SWEDISH LINEN: Size 16/2 (top) showing double twist.
  (b). SLUB LINEN: Note slub on left.
8. KNOX LINEN TWIST: Size 14 (showing regularity of twist).
9. FINE LINEN THREADS: Very strong (showing size only).

Enlarged photographs of these threads will be found on page 13.

fibre drawn out to make 840 yards of yarn; the thickness or size is known as No. 1 count. If the yarn is drawn out further, so that 1 pound makes twice 840 yards it is known as count No. 2. As the count numbers rise the yarn gets finer.

This standard base of 1 pound is used for cotton, linen and wool.

Cotton 1 pound of 1s count cotton = 840 yards
Linen 1 pound of 1s linen = 300 yards
Wool has two measurements:
    Worsted yarn—1 pound of 1s = 560 yards
    Woollen yarn—1 pound of 1s = 256 yards

PLY YARNS: When two or more strands or yarns are twisted together they are called ply yarns. They are called 2-ply, 3-ply and so on, according to the number used in their construction. A single yarn may be of good quality; but where durability is important ply yarns are preferable. Warps are stronger if made of ply yarns or alternated with ply and single yarns.

Yarn construction and yarn count are expressed in the following manner. The term 1/30s denotes the use of a single yarn having a yarn count of 30. In the same way 3/30s denotes the use of a 3-ply yarn, that is, three strands twisted together, each having a separate yarn count of 30. A 3-ply yarn indicated by 3/30s would be the equivalent to a single yarn having a count of 10. In the same way, 2/10s (containing two single strands of 10s) is equivalent in size to 1/5s. To work out the quantities of yarn it is necessary to know the count, i.e.—

1. 5 lb of 3/18s cotton, divide 3 into 18 then multiply $5 \times 6 \times 840 = 25{,}200$ yards.

2. 8 oz of 2/28 worsted, divide 2 into 28 $\dfrac{14 \times 560}{2}$ = 3,920 yards.

3. 10 lb of 19s woollen $10 \times 19 \times 256 = 48{,}640$ yards.

4. 6 lb of 2/16s linen $6 \times 8 \times 300 = 14{,}400$ yards.

If the count number is not known, take a piece of hardboard and make it 18 inches long by 4 inches wide. Wrap the yarn around it lengthwise, remembering once round is one yard, wrap enough yards to make 1 oz, keeping careful count of the number of yards that are being put on the scales. Multiply the number of yards it has taken to make 1 oz by 16—you then have the number of yards per pound of that particular yarn.

SPINNING A WORSTED YARN: The very best quality wools are made into worsted yarn. Each fibre must have a good staple length. Commercial yarns are carded and combed and are tightly twisted, making a much stronger, finer, smoother yarn. In making a homespun worsted keep the fibres straight and parallel by drawing out the fibres from the bottom end of the staple nearest the shearer's cut.

(Right) LONG STAPLE: Not carded—ready to be spun into a "worsted homespun", with the fibres coming from the staples in their long lengths.

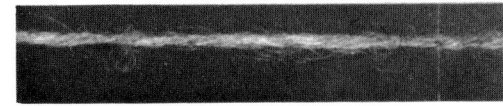

HOMESPUN WORSTED: The long fibres are drawn out and twisted in the spinning process, giving less fluffiness.

MACHINESPUN WORSTED: Compact, even, and trimmed.

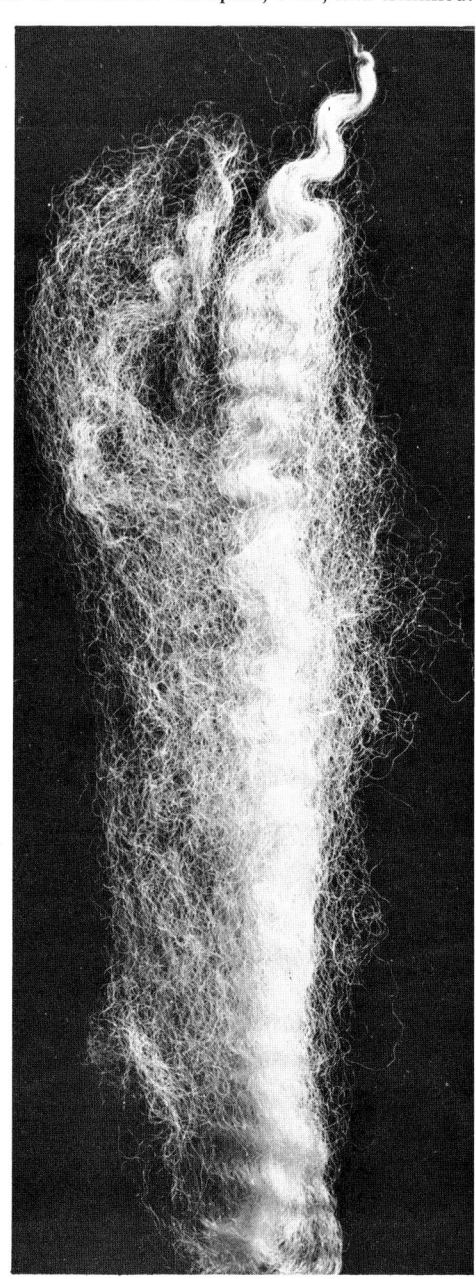

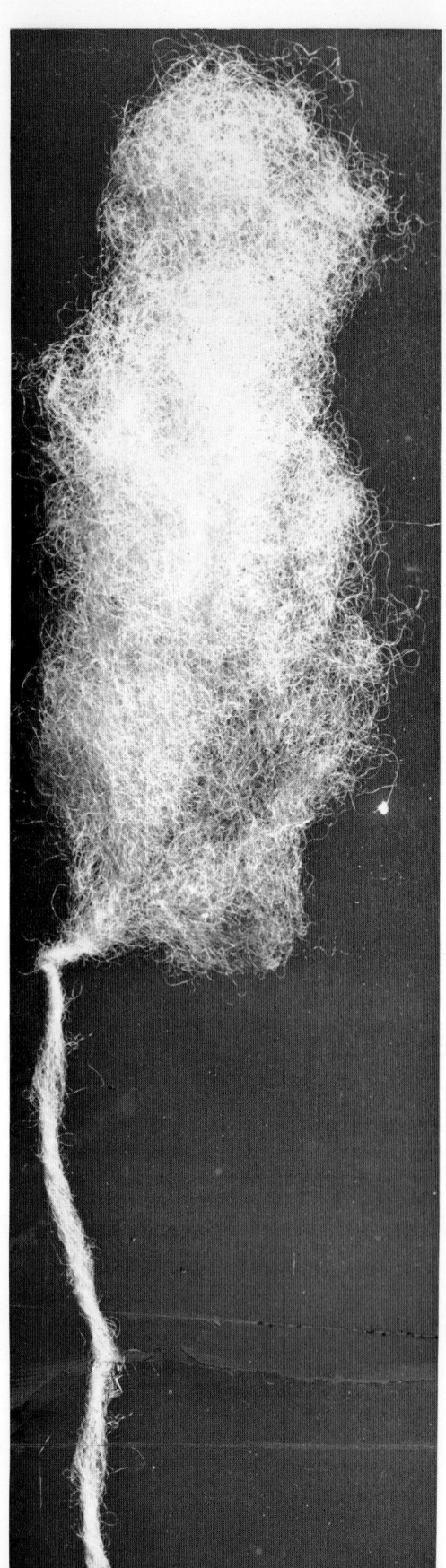

SPINNING A WOOLLEN YARN: Woollen yarn is made of the short fibres. They are carded only and are not so tightly twisted. Therefore the yarn is weaker, bulkier, more spongy to touch and the twist is less even.

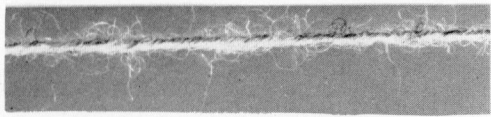

HOMESPUN WOOLLEN: The home-carded rolags spun into a more fluffy yarn.

MACHINESPUN WOOLLEN: More open in character and springy.

(Left) SHORT FIBRES: Carded wool—homespun woollen. Here the fibres have been carded and opened out and rolled. They do not lie in straight lengths as they were grown on the sheep's back.

SELECTING COMMERCIAL YARNS FOR WARP THREADS

In weaving, the warp threads that run the length of the loom are under tension and take the strain of the beating, so they must be reasonably strong and still be a decorative part of the finished product. They are all-important and must be well planned.

Certain threads mix in a warp better than others due to the difference in the amount of elasticity. Cotton in comparison with wool is slightly stronger but not as elastic, so, to keep the tension of the warp even, use either an all-cotton warp with a wool weft, or ply cotton and wool together and make the warp of this combination. Being of like threads (i.e. wool and cotton warp with a wool weft) this latter combination will look better than an all-cotton warp with an all-wool weft. A mixed warp of a few cotton and a few wool threads will have an uneven tension and will be more difficult to deal with. This is also true of linen, which will sag if there is any unevenness of tension.

The following commercial yarns for which enlarged photographs are given opposite offer some suggestions.

1. GIMPS: Showing very hard twist on the two top threads in comparison with the bottom thread All these make strong warp threads.
2. COTTON THREADS: Two sizes, *top*, 16/6; bottom, 8/8—very strong but loose twist for soft yarns.
3. MILL COTTON: *Top*. A group of fine strands not twisted. *Below*. A group of four slightly thicker strands—loose.
4. ENSIGN LACING: A very tightly twisted fisherman's cord, 16/12. Suitable for warp threads for floor rugs but too harsh for material weaving.
5. LINEN FLAX SEAMING TWINE: Two sizes—very strong clean stripped fibre in natural colouring. Both make a firm foundation for any type of woven floor rug.
6. LINEN LOCKSTITCH: Size 2/7 cord with an S twist and a shiny finish. A good weaving cord.
7. SWEDISH LINENS: 16/2, (a) slub, (b) (use simply on 8 or 10 dent reed).
8. KNOX LINEN: Twist No. 14.
9. FINE LINENS: All are good strong threads for warping with pleasing results.

4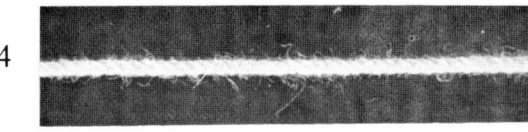

5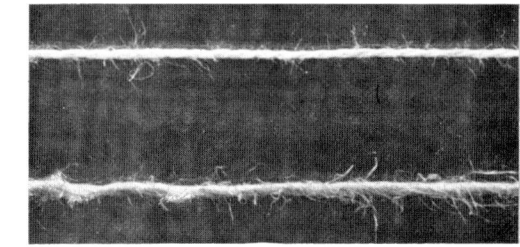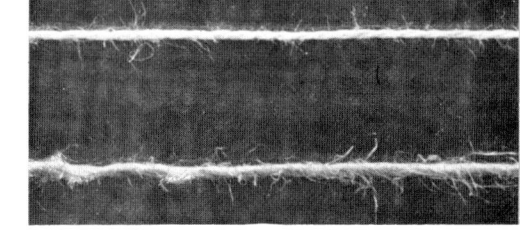

6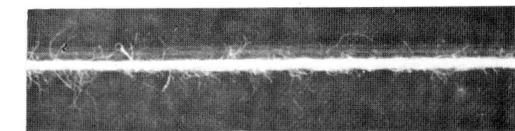

7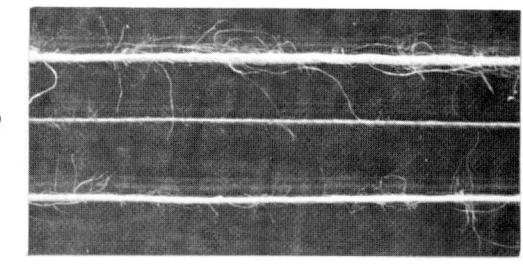

1

2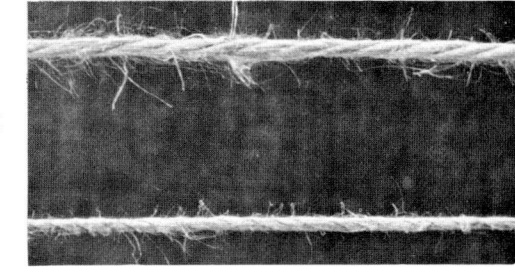

8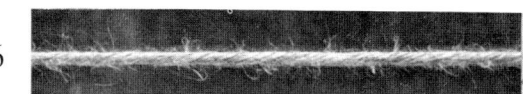

3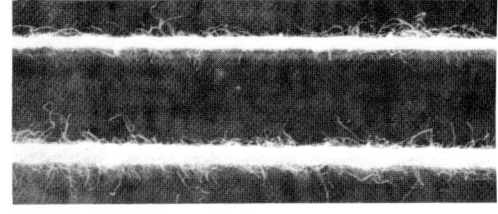

9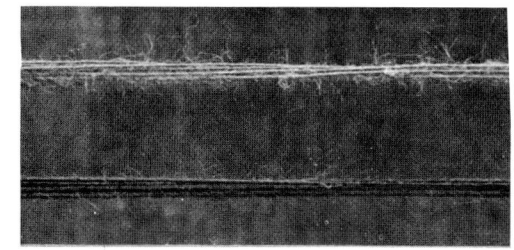

WOOL YARNS FOR WARP THREADS: Any wool yarn is ideal for warp threads and even the finest of yarns when under tension is strong and springy. It mixes well with silk, alternating threads of silk and wool. A single-ply homespun is difficult to handle if sufficient twist has not made a strong enough thread. Ply a fine worsted wool or a chemical fibre to give that extra strength. The following illustrations show but a few of many combinations. The threads in the photographs are enlarged approximately 1½ times.

5

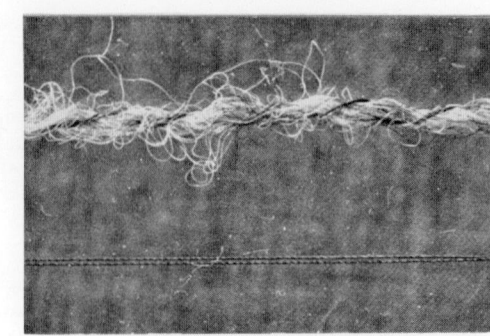

6

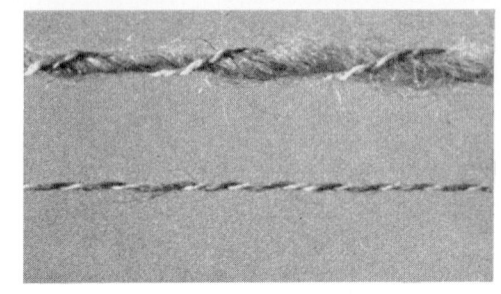

1

2

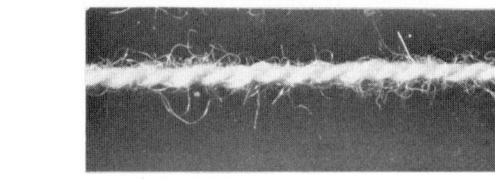

7

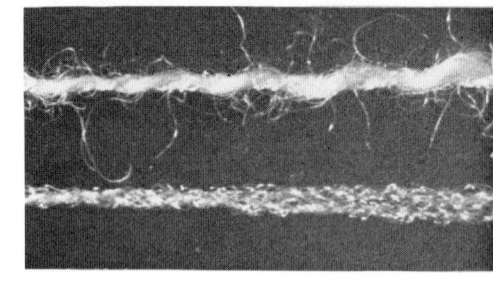

3

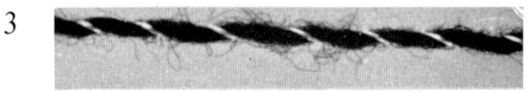

4

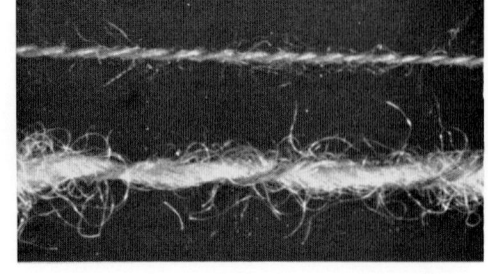

1. Machine-spun wool threads of varying sizes strong enough for wool threads and suitable to weave fine dress fabrics.
2. A thicker wool yarn for upholstery material.
3. A wool and rayon mixture (commercial thread), would weave into a strong tweed fabric or upholstery.
4. White homespun thread plyed with fine worsted thread adding colour and strength.
5. Grey homespun wool plyed with synthetic coloured-sheer threads adding colour and strength.
6. Off-white homespun wool plyed with flake linen thread for texture.
7. White homespun plyed with white sheen polyester for shine and slight glitter effect.

Examples 4, 5, 6, and 7 show plying homespun threads with commercial threads to add *strength* to homespun single-ply wools; to add *colour*, or to emphasise some *textural* effect.

HOW TO USE EFFECT YARNS FOR VARIATION: These can be used in the warp if care is taken in denting them wisely. Indeed, they often make a unique fabric and, therefore, are well worth seeking.

The five examples shown on this page have been photographed natural size (on the left) and enlarged (right) to show clearly the characteristic detail of each effect yarn.

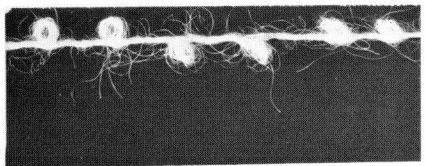 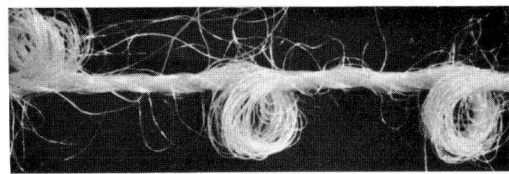

1. Loop yarn—wool and synthetic.

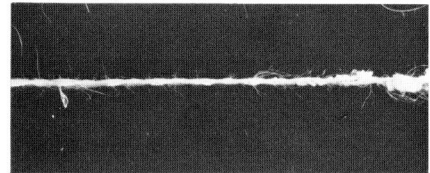 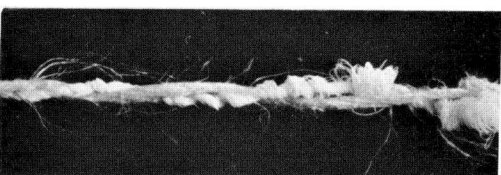

2. Flake yarn.

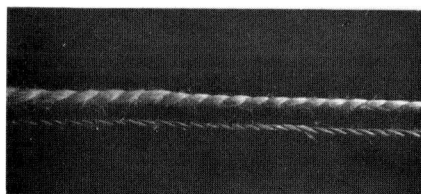 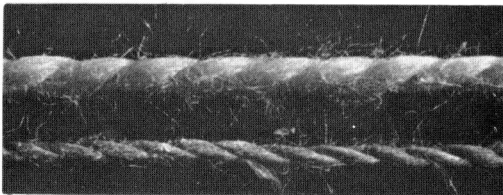

3. Mercerised cotton.

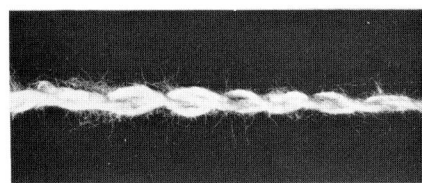 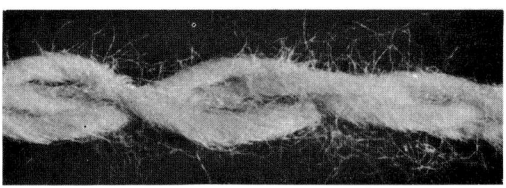

4. Cotton/nylon 5-ply.

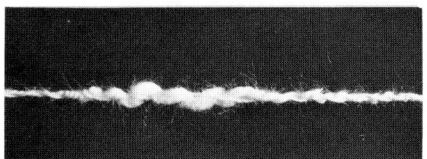 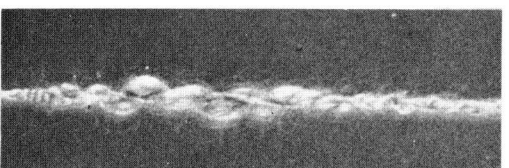

5. Thick and thin novelty.

Chapter 2

KNITTING WITH HOMESPUN WOOL

IS MY homespun wool equivalent to a 2- or 3- or 4-ply, or a double knit or triple knit, and which of the novelty yarns? Here are some samples for comparison with your own spinning.

Spinners who are constantly at their wheels soon develop such a fine even thread that it becomes difficult for them to spin a novelty yarn for a slub effect. Grade your homespun as soon as you become a consistent spinner and you will have a wide range of knitting patterns from which to make a selection.

An average man's jersey for wearing on more "dressy" occasions will take 27–30 oz of homespun wool of the thickness shown on the stitch gauge sample on page 18.

A bulkie or a "Sloppy Joe", depending on the wearer's size and the degree of sloppiness desired, can take up to 40 oz and, because of their weight, these garments have a tendency to stretch and fall after laundering. In contrast, a lightweight open mesh "shell" suitable for wearing with a woman's suit and knitted in single-ply homespun (as shown on page 21) weighs 4 to 5 oz completed. A women's long-sleeved jersey should weigh about 12 to 15 oz.

A good fleece weighing from 8 to 10 lb after skirting should yield enough spun wool to make three, or possibly four average-sized jerseys (not the "Sloppy Joe" variety). This is assuming that the fleece is of even coloration throughout.

HOMESPUN COMPARED WITH MACHINE-KNIT WOOLS

Nos 1, 2, 3 and 4 are homespun whereas Nos 5 to 9 are machinespun by well known knit-wool manufacturers:

1. Single-ply homespun.
2. 2-ply homespun with a soft twist.
3. Homespun thick 2-ply.
4. Very fine 2-ply homespun.
5. Medium spun 4-ply knitwool.
6. Medium spun double crepe.
7. Medium spun quickerknit.
8. Medium spun doubleknit.
9. Medium spun carpetknit.

All the homespun threads photographed were soft and fluffy like mohair wools. The single-ply homespun was a strong thread not easily broken and light in weight. In thickness it compared with a 3-ply machine wool. Single-ply spun much finer than this lacked strength, and when more twist was added to .gain strength the thread became harsh. The fleece wool used was a fine crossbred Romney of good spinning qualities.

Average 2-ply homespun proved to be thicker than 4-ply and ranked with the double crepe, quickerknit and doubleknit in the sample machine-wools chosen.

Thick 2-ply homespun was thicker than average carpet wools, whereas very fine 2-ply homespun Merino thread was only slightly thicker than 40 sewing cotton.

SIZE OF NEEDLES. The following is a guide but not a hard-and-fast rule:

2- or 3-ply require a fine needle: 12, 11, 10.
4-ply or doubleknit: 9, 8.
Tripleknit: 6, 5.

How to Compare British and American Knitting-Needle Sizes

British:	13	12	11	10	9	8	7	6	5	4	3	2	1	0
American:	0	1	2	3	4	5	6	7	8	9	10	11	12	13

Notice that to the American needle size you add the number that will equal 13. The number you add will be the British number. For example No. 2 American corresponds with 11 British (2 + 11 = 13); No. 8 American is No. 5 British (8 + 5 = 13). Note that very large sizes vary; these should be checked before purchasing.

KNITTING-NEEDLE SIZE GAUGE. It is advisable to keep one of these with your knitting-needle supply box—every yarn shop sells them. With frequent use the size numbers marked on the needle itself often become worn and unreadable. For checking the size, slip the needle well down into whatever hole allows the needle to slip up and down easily. This will identify the size.

STITCH GAUGE. Always knit a sample in plain stitch *no matter what patterned stitch you have chosen for the garment. It is the most important part of knitting.* This

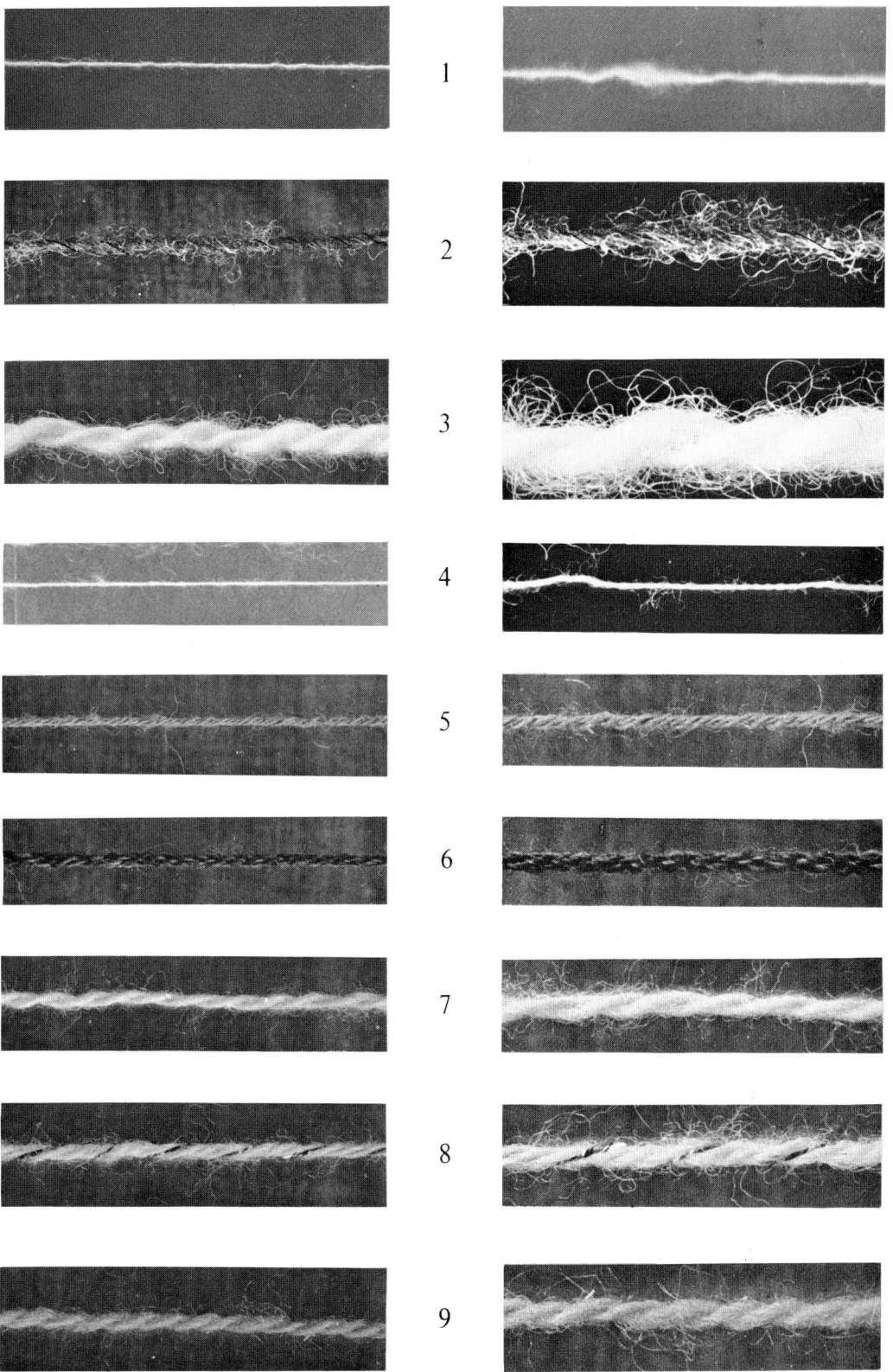

1

2

3

4

5

6

7

8

9

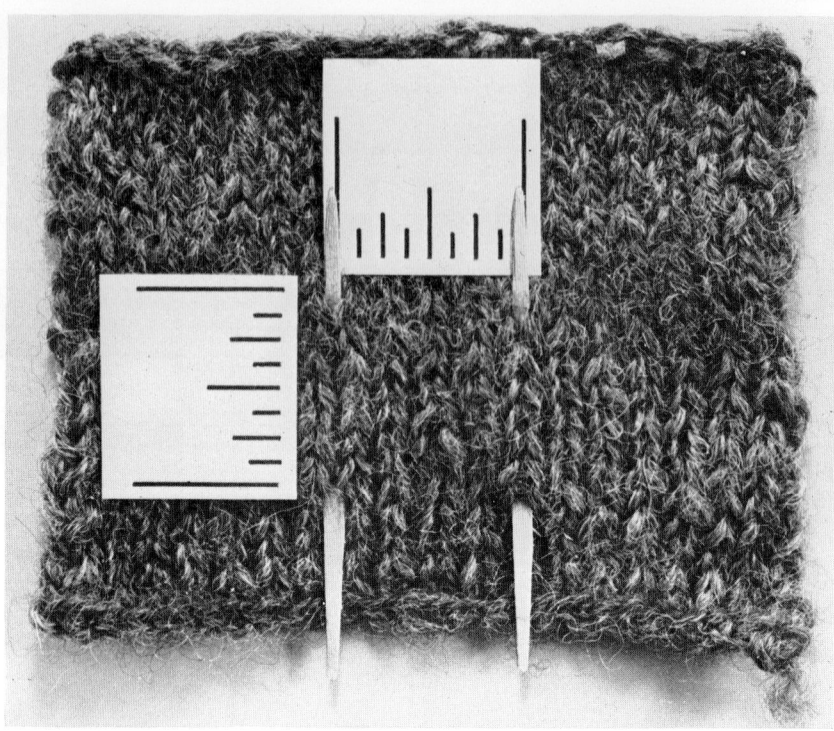

A stitch gauge showing 7 stitches to one inch.

sample will enable you to measure how many stitches to the inch and how many rows to the inch. There are so many variables with which to contend—not only the thinness or thickness of the homespun wool yarn and the size of knitting needles, but also the individual knitter, whether she be a loose or a tight knitter.

If your knitting is too tight you are getting more stitches per inch than the gauge calls for. Change to a larger needle.

If you are getting fewer stitches per inch, your knitting is too loose, so change to a smaller needle.

It does not matter what needle size is used so long as the gauge is correct.

HOW TO MAKE YOUR STITCH GAUGE. (See photograph at top of page.) Stocking stitch, i.e. K1 row, P1 row, on straight needles; knit every row on circular needles— this is the standard stitch gauge and all homespun wools should be tested on patterns planned for a stocking stitch gauge.

Cast on 20 stitches (K1 row, P1 row) for 20 rows; press the sample. Now take a standard ruler and count how many stitches make 1 in.; how many rows of knitting make 1 in. Make the calculations in the middle of the sample, not from the cast-on edge as casting-on can be either very tight or very loose, depending on the knitter and her method. Be very accurate in counting the number of stitches to the square inch as even half a stitch when multiplied by the required measurements of the garment will make a difference of from 6 to 10 stitches. This will alter the fit of the garment.

MAKING A BASIC PATTERN

I prefer to make my basic pattern from an old sheet so that as I knit I can test my measurements on it; then, when steam-pressing each knitted section, I can pin them to the basic pattern and press both together, thus avoiding any stretching of the knitting.

The diagrams on the right will show where to take the necessary measurements:

FRONT: (a) Centre front. (b) Shoulder. (c) Across the front—take three measurements approx. $2\frac{1}{2}$ in. from top of shoulder. (d) Bust measurements. (e) Same as for back. (f) Armhole. (g) Same as for back—to correspond. (h) For V neckline.
BACK: (a) Centre back. (b) Shoulder. (c) Across the back—take three measurements—approx. $2\frac{1}{2}$ in. down from shoulder. (d) Under arm, where sleeve will join. (e) Bottom of garment. (f) Armhole. (g) From under arm to bottom of garment.
SLEEVE: (i) Top of sleeve to cuff. (j) Under arm to cuff. (k) Across the wide part of sleeve where it will join with back and front. (l) Width at cuff.

HOW TO PRESS YOUR KNITTING: Place knitted sections right side up on the pressing board; carefully pin on your basic pattern, originally cut out of old sheeting, and make your knitting sections correspond. They should do so without stretching unduly. Steam with a moderately hot iron. For mixed yarns use a moderately warm iron in case your mixture of yarns contains a synthetic which does not stand heat. Be very careful

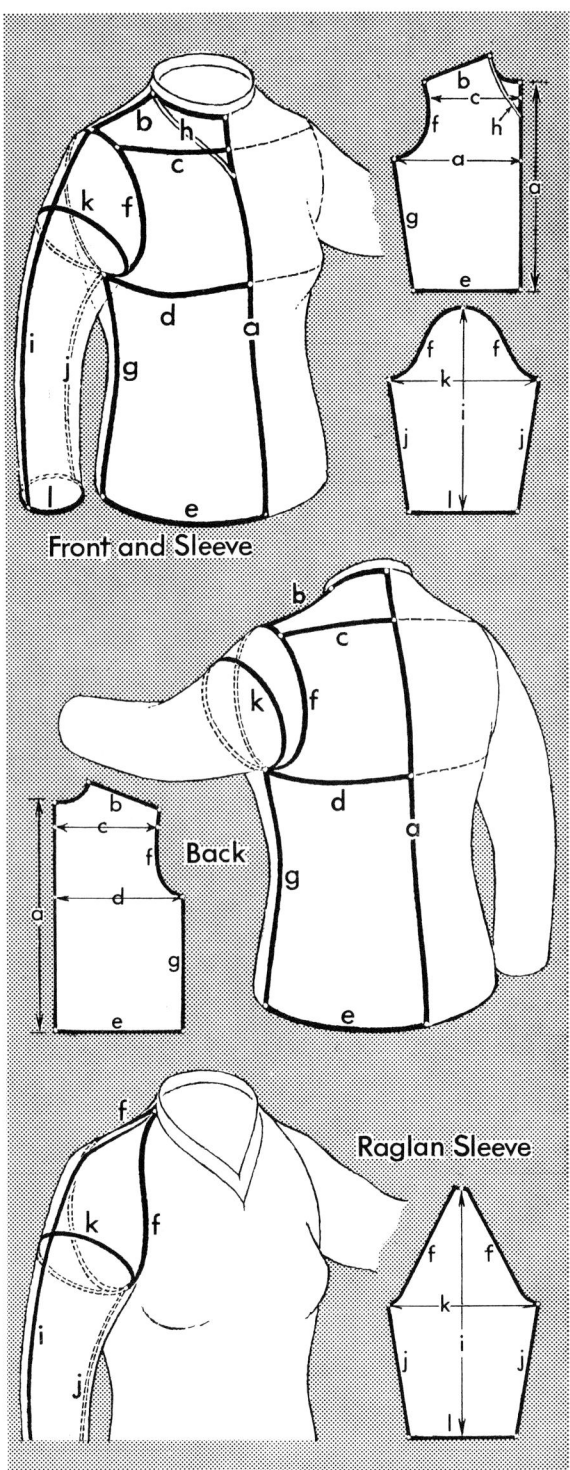

Front and Sleeve

Back

Raglan Sleeve

not to rest the weight of the iron on any one spot. Do not apply too much pressure on iron. With ribbing patterns, press only lightly.

When dry, some light pressing may be required on the right side. This will depend on appearance and pattern.

Sew up garment and press seams flat, with sufficient pressure on the iron to open the seams without marking.

FAIRISLE PATTERNS
FOR HOMESPUN WOOLS

Hand spinners dealing with the delightful shades of natural wools and the plant-dyed colours that blend so attractively with the natural often require patterns that shade well together in fairisle. The Shetland Island knitters are noted for their high standard of achievement in their "fern" patterns used either as bands around the waist or as yoke designs, or as a centre panel for a sweater. The detailed graphs can be followed as such on either 2-needle knitting or circular knitting. As previously advised, make your stitch gauge in stocking stitch and your body measurements in sheeting material, but now you will need a 2 in. – 4 in. sample in the fairisle pattern, shading your wools to make a harmonious blend.

By filling all her stitch gauge samples and patterned samples a knitter soon builds up an adequate reference file which saves considerable time and is a further check on stitch gauge adjustments for her particular style of knitting.

Any of the graphed patterns of traditional Maori taaniko weaving published in *The Art of Taaniko Weaving*, by S. M. Mead (pages 64–71) are recommended for experimentation.

Sooner or later an enterprising knitter will prefer to make her own fairisle designs, thus developing a wider range of colour combinations for both natural and home-dyed wools as well as to reproduce in knitting the wealth of traditional designs indigenous to most countries. Buy some graph paper or rule it up yourself—10 squares to the inch is a good size.

Work out your design, using a different symbol for each of the different colours to be used. To avoid making any mistakes enter the number of rows at the side of your graph paper and have a key chart for your symbols to correspond with each colour.

Count also the number of stitches in one complete pattern and calculate how many patterns can be worked in a row, and how many stitches may have to be "fitted in" at either end.

For example, if one pattern contains 12 stitches and there are 100 on the needle, there will be 8 complete patterns and 2 stitches at either end to be knitted in the basic colour.

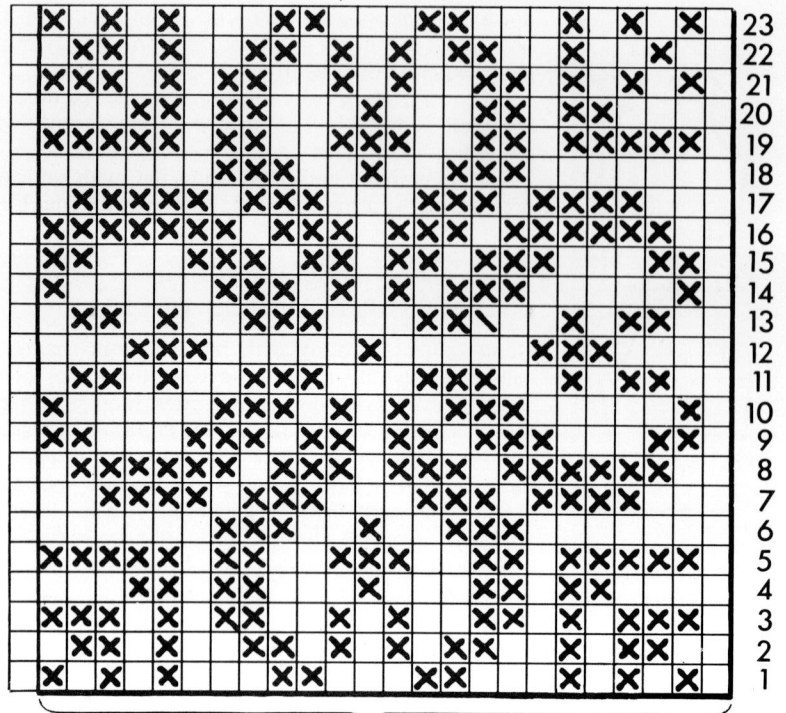

Repeat these 24 stitches

An example of the Shetland
Island Fern pattern.

An example of a fairisle pattern with a multiple of 12 stitches.
Twenty-three rows complete this design.

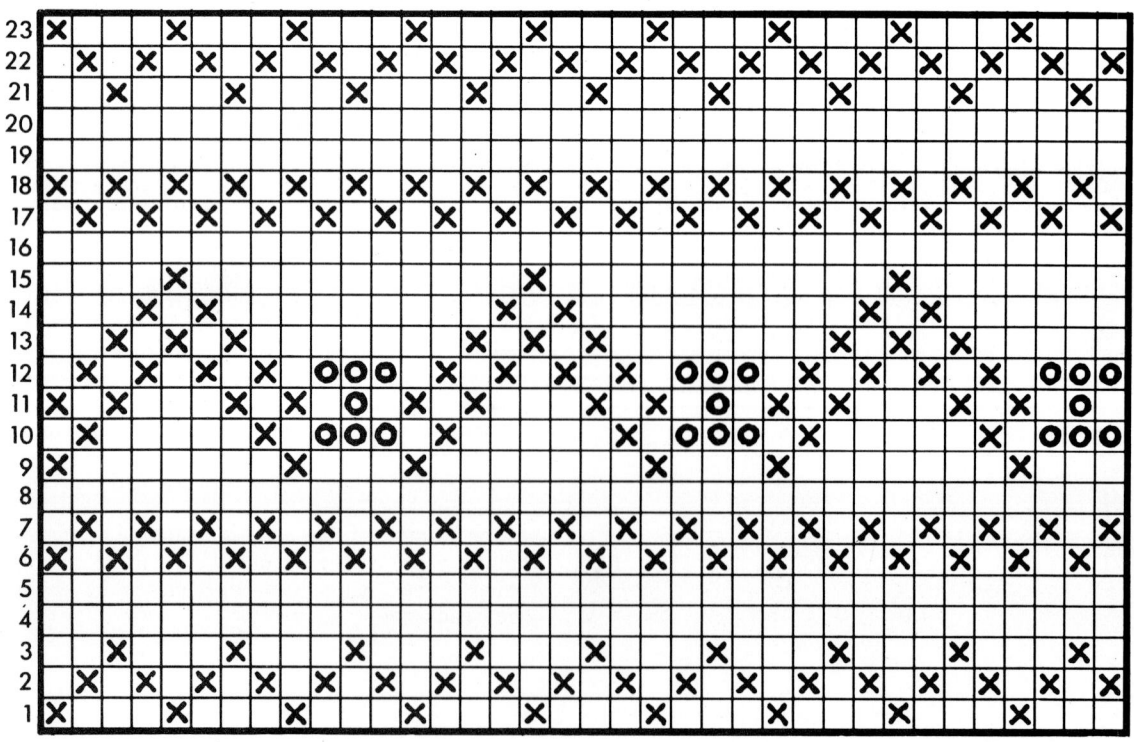

KNITTING WITH SINGLE-PLY HOMESPUN WOOL

For certain effects and for lightweight jerseys a single-ply thread is quite strong enough if sufficient twist is applied in the spinning. For this, select your wool carefully so as to achieve a strong yet soft thread. Crochet motifs, lace edgings, Irish crochet netting, all with their variations can be made with homespun threads either single-ply or 2-ply according to the required weight of the finished product and the pattern stitch selected.

A lacy pattern will not work well with a heavy type of spun yarn, neither would a bold cable stitch give the desired appearance in either a single-ply yarn or a fine 2-ply merino wool spun as finely as a 40-size cotton sewing thread.

Two examples of this are shown in the photography.

Gauge: 9 stitches = 2 in.
8 rows of pattern = 1½ in.

Pattern Stitch:
Row 1: +purl the next st, wrapping yarn around needle twice, repeat from + across row.
Row 2: +knit the next stitch, dropping extra wrap off needle to form long st, repeat from + across row.
Rows 3, 4 and 6: purl.
Rows 5, 7 and 8: knit.
Repeat these 8 rows for pattern stitch.

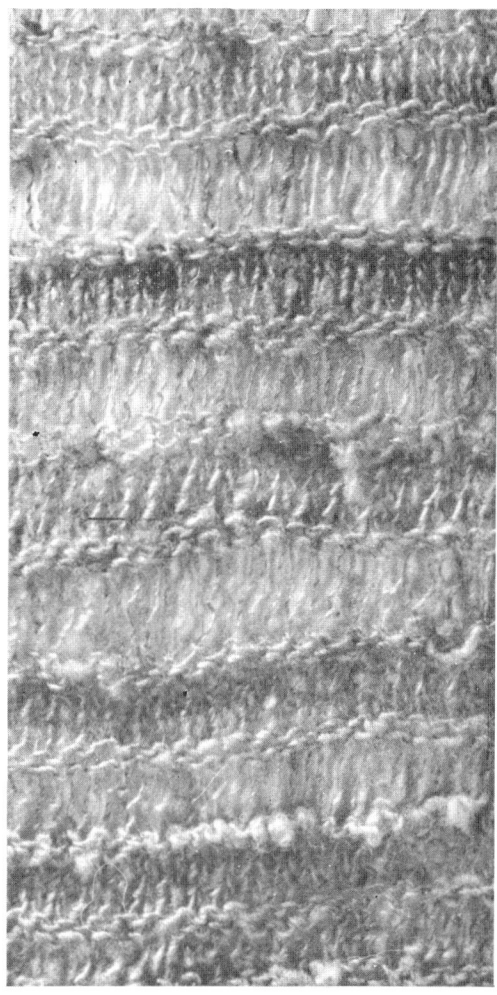

Top: Pattern to show the texture and the type of pattern stitch to apply to fine single-ply homespun.

Left: Lace knitting for a baby's shawl. This shawl, 52 inches square, spun and knitted by Mrs McPhail of Waipaoa, Gisborne, New Zealand, has a total weight of 3¾ oz.

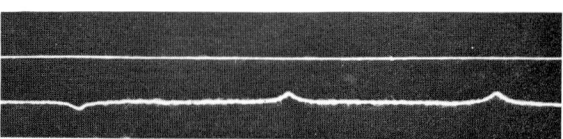

Size 40 sewing thread *top,* and 2-ply homespun *below,* compared.

Chapter 3

WEAVING WITH WOOL YARNS

ONCE AGAIN, planning and sampling are all-important. A fine worsted wool yarn makes a strong warp: even though it looks fragile, the elasticity of the yarn and the extra number of fine threads per inch under tension make the overall warp strong. The balance of wool warp and wool weft makes a pleasing fabric and the fine yarns are usually set 2 per dent—24 ends per inch. Mixed warps of thick and thin are a variation—also textured yarns spaced with plain to form a check.

A tight tension on a wool warp in a close set will enable the weft to be beaten extremely lightly, thus making a softer woven cloth. Handspun used in the warp must be evenly spun and of stronger tension than that spun for the weft. An over-twisted handspun will make a harsh fabric, hence the great importance of sampling.

When winding the warp forward to each new weaving position, any textured threads may carry the Heddle frames forward. Move the frames back in position before finally tightening the tension.

Homespun wool makes a good weft. It can be woven singly or plied with other wool, cotton, or synthetic yarns. There are many alternatives. Plain weave shows the character of homespun wool to a greater advantage than a much-patterned weave.

Always weave with your stretcher about $\frac{1}{2}$ in. – $1\frac{1}{2}$ in.

Handwoven coating material enlarged to show the weft threads—2 rows of wool loop followed by 2 rows of fine wool thread, the 4 rows in white (see opposite page for directions).

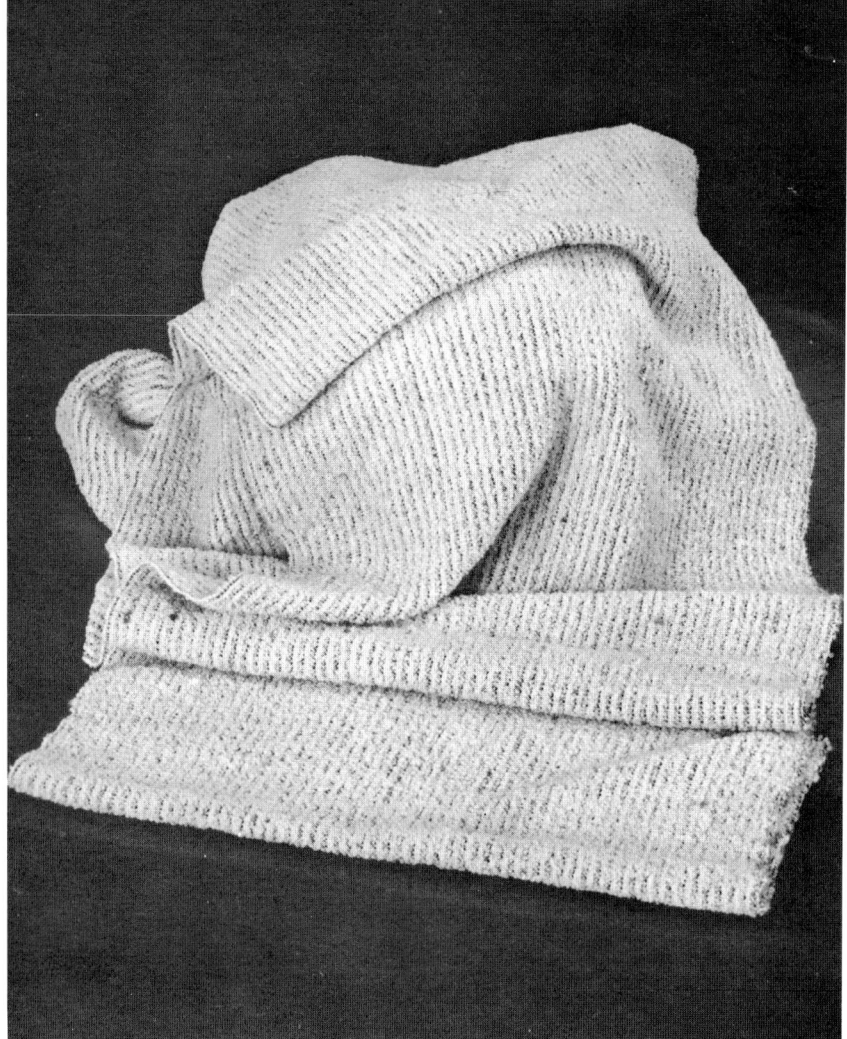

Threading tie-up (threading from left to right of loom).

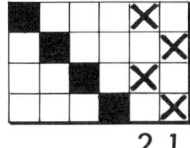

2 1

Handwoven coating material with warp threads making a stripe of black, grey, fawn and white. On the same warp, using a more gentle pull on the beater would make a more open fabric suitable for a dress material.

from the last weft shot; leave a good arc, and then your material should not pull in unduly.

A weaving stretcher (also called a temple) is a large adjustable slideruler with brads at each end to catch into the edges of the woven fabric.

If homespun wool in the warp shows any tendency to fluff and stick to the adjoining warp ends, mix some cornflour with cold water, enough to make a thick paste (do not cook it!) and dab this on to the warp ends. When dry, continue weaving. The cornflour will readily wash out when you wash and press the material after it comes off the loom.

WEAVING COATING MATERIAL

WARP: Wool black, grey, fawn white.
WEFT: 2 shots of loop white.
2 shots of plain white.

WARP ENDS: 576.
ENDS TO THE INCH: 24.
REED: 12.
DENTING: 2 per dent.
PATTERN THREADING: tabby, i.e. 1, 2, 3, 4 for 4-shaft looms.
1, 2 for 2 shafts.
TREADLING: pedal 1 corresponds to levers 1 + 3 on table loom (4-shaft).
pedal 2 corresponds to levers 2 + 4 on table loom (4-shaft).
REQUIREMENTS PER YARD: 6–8 oz for both warp and weft.

Note: This is a reliable setting for many materials—but select finer warp threads for suiting and dress materials. Learn to throw a boat shuttle instead of a shuttle stick to make good even material.

Boat-shaped shuttles and roller shuttles are hollowed out to hold a piece of 10- or 12-gauge wire on which is wound the weft thread. The end of the thread passes through an opening in the side or from the end. In throwing the shuttle through the shed opening, it skids rapidly along the warp threads close to the reed and is caught with the other hand, the shed changed, and the shuttle thrown back to be caught again. It is this rhythmical action of throwing and catching that makes an even weave.

Too much loop wool in the weft would make the fabric look too spongy.

It is quite possible to weave material on a 24 in. table loom in sufficient yardage for a suit or coat. You will find it cuts very economically. Just increase your yardage to about 8½ or 9 yards, depending on the size required. A skirt-length will be twice the distance from the waistline to the hemline.

The yarns shown on page 14 have been selected as suitable for warp threads, which present more of a problem than weft threads because of the strain and tension on warps. By and large, any type of thread can be used for weft, depending on the purpose of the woven article. In planning your sample weave remember that a correct balance of like-threads in warp and weft will be more pleasing. This applies to colour combinations as well as threads.

WEAVING A PONCHO

WARP: Wool, blue 2 shades turquoise 2 shades grey.
WEFT: Handspun grey plyed with flake linen.
WARP ENDS: 468.
ENDS TO THE INCH: 12.
REED: No. 12.
DENTING: 1 per dent.

PATTERN: Mock leno 2 in. and tabby stripe 1½ in. Threading as on graph paper chart shown below.
TREADLING: As on graph paper chart below.
REQUIREMENTS: 6–8 oz for warp and weft. Weave 2½ yards for the following pattern.

TO MAKE THE PONCHO. Cut yourself a standard pattern piece from old sheeting to the dimensions shown on the diagram at the foot of this page (this represents the finished size):

Place standard pattern on woven material—allow ¾ in.–1 in. all round for seams. With a zigazg stitch on your sewing machine zigzag around the 4 edges. This will prevent any fraying of material. Press while pattern sheeting is still pinned in place. Now remove sheeting pattern and cut another 3 pieces the same as above, taking care to match the stripe for the centre back and the centre front. Zigzag and press as before.

Join centre front sections. Press flat and oversew edges.
Join centre back sections. Press flat and oversew edges.
Sew in 8 in. zip on left-hand shoulder seam.
Sew shoulder seams. Press seams flat and over-sew as before.

Cut out roll collar to fit. Join the two end sections.
Press before joining to neck edge and bind with bias binding.

The roll collar can be finished with button and button-hole to fit snugly into the neck. Make a fringe around the lower edges with homespun wool the same as the weft threads in the weaving.

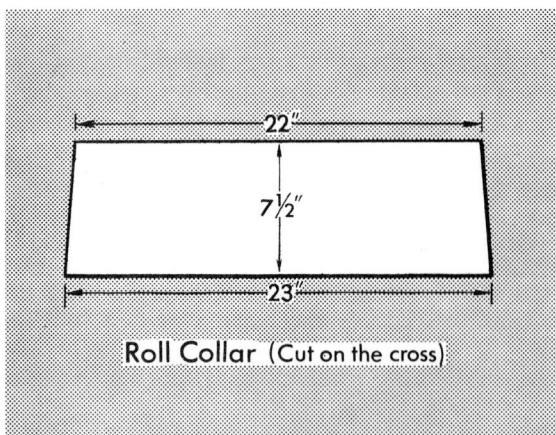

Roll Collar (Cut on the cross)

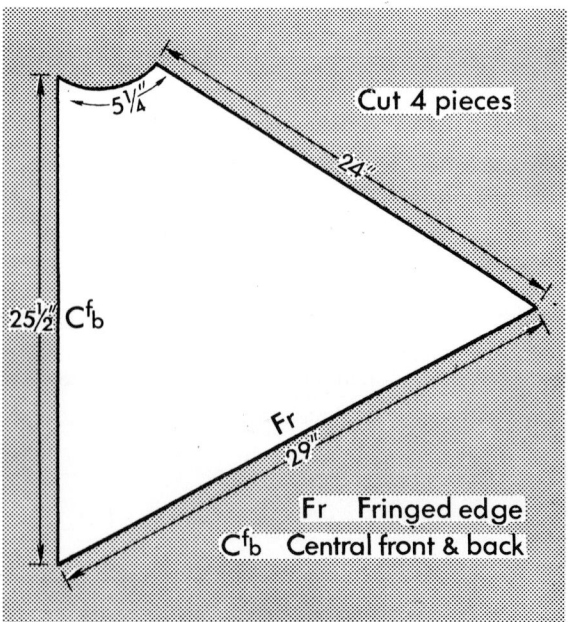

Fr Fringed edge
Cᶠb Central front & back

24

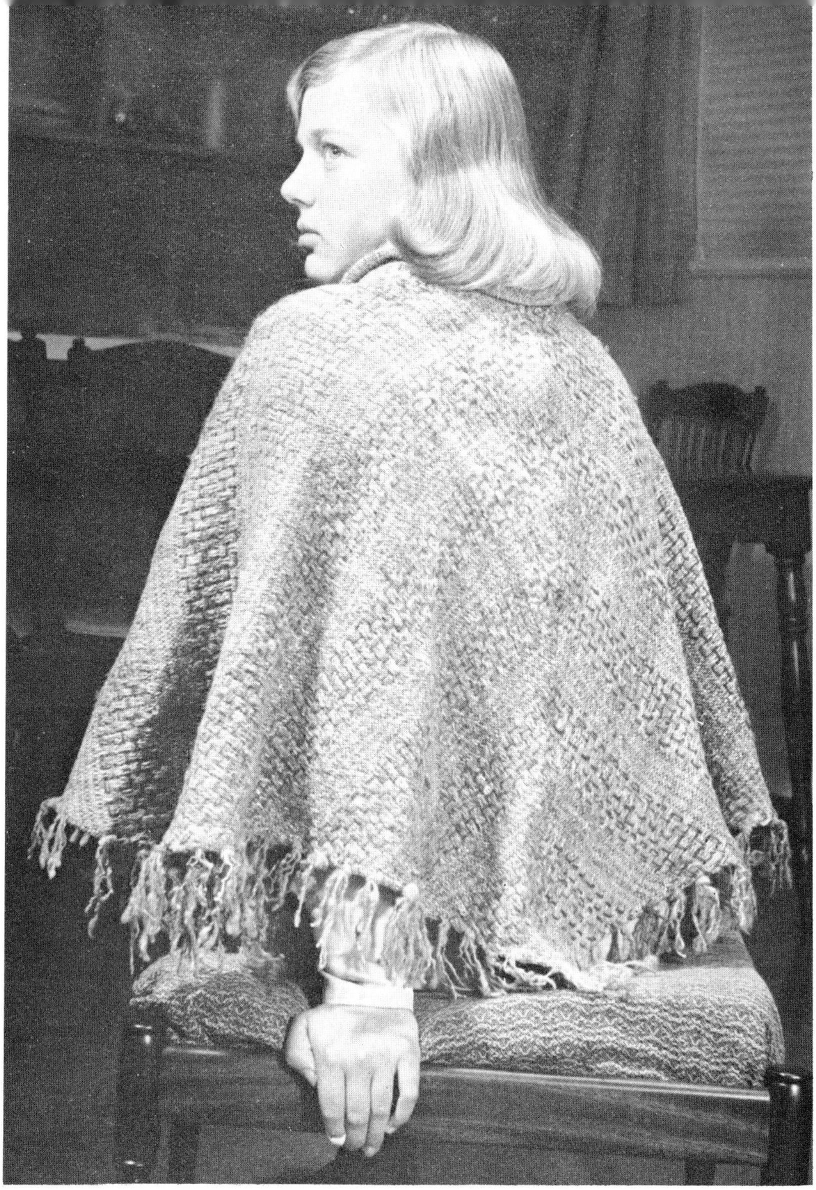

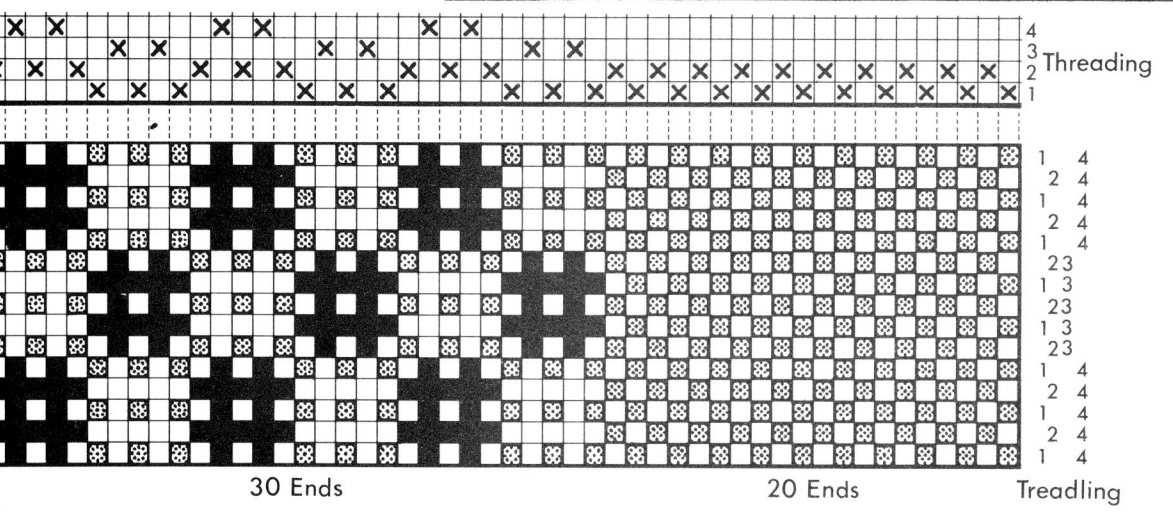

Open weave Poncho,
handwoven by the author.

4
3
2
1
Threading
1 4
2 4
1 4
2 4
1 4
23
1 3
23
1 3
23
1 4
2 4
1 4
2 4
1 4
30 Ends
20 Ends
Treadling

Chapter 4

DEALING WITH AVERAGE AND INFERIOR WOOLS

SO FAR this book has advocated selecting and using the very best wools that will amply reward the craftsman for his handmade product. But by using only the best there is much wastage of material by spinners; industry cannot afford this wastage, neither can the home craftsman.

The home answer to the problem, as in industry, lies in blending, i.e. using these lower-grade wools in combination with selected long-stapled, well crimped good wool. Length and tensile strength influence the spinning quality of any fibre—long fibres, fully "sound" throughout their length, make for good spinning, e.g. hair, jute, flax fibres will all spin well but probably lack the "style" or crimp that good fleece wool has to offer. However, not all wool comes up to this standard but, nevertheless, can and should be used if wastage and expense are to be avoided.

Wools are described largely by the breed of sheep that produce them with further details of the fibre diameter called *count* or sometimes *quality*. (The word quality must not be confused with *style* as in the wool trade quality only means measurement of fibre diameter and not the assessment of the material. Style on the other hand refers to the characteristics of fibre in consideration of length, crimping, colour and strength.)

Wools of good "style" can be described as those having good staple length, with even and well defined crimping from butt to tip. Good colour and soundness (freedom from "break" or "tenderness") combine with length and crimp to give style. Good wool comes from the body of the sheep which is genetically able to produce these desirable characteristics in its wool, and which has been well bred, fed, and cared for. The body wool of a sheep excludes wools from the neck, belly, and legs (or "points").

On these parts of a sheep the wool differs from the body wool. The neck wool is finer and softer, and has the properties of flannel. It is often longer but can appear short and fluffy and will probably contain foreign matter such as dust, seeds and burrs, and other vegetable matter. The belly wool from the underside of a sheep, is curly, thicker and "springy", and appears shorter than the body wool, though in actual fact belly wool is often long and well developed and can be combed out to give a sound fibre which will give "pile" to a woven article. It is often discoloured, specially if off a male sheep, but the stain caused by urine is generally confined to the middle area and can be removed to leave a large quantity of clean fibre.

Wool from the legs or points is generally shorter, thicker, and carries more condition (grease and sweat) than the body wools. It is often discoloured and can vary greatly in length—first pieces from higher up the leg being up to 5 in. in length and second pieces being the shorter from the lower leg to 1½ inches in length.

All these wools are known as fleece oddments, but are referred to by name: necks, bellies, and pieces. They create a problem for the home spinner and are often discarded as unusable. This is a pity, and a great waste of raw material. Some processing is required to bring them into use—it may take a little time, but the craftsman will be well rewarded for the trouble. They should certainly not be shunned as low-grade wools. It must be made clear at this stage that there *are* low-grade wools which should be avoided when choosing material for spinning. These are self-evident if the hand craftsman knows what faults to look for.

Do not choose wools that are:

1. Thin, wasty and tender when pulled for testing tensile strength. The fibre can be short—down to 1½ inches—but it must be "sound" along its length with no "break". However, in some long wools there may be a break near the butt or near the tip; provided the fibre between these "breaks" is sound and gives enough length to spin, it should not be discarded.
2. Tightly cotted or matted. These wools are hopeless to handle and need heavy carding with great fibre loss before they can be spun.
3. Badly stained by yolk or urine. These wools will not wash out white. Yolk-stained wools can be dyed, but shade variations will occur.
4. Wools that contain seed and burrs—these foreign bodies are hard to remove other than by processes that are beyond the facilities of the home craftsman.

In general you can expect to get good fleece oddments from good quality, clean fleeces and these should be blended into the body wools during the process of spinning. By doing so the nature of the yarns can be changed, with interesting results. A more detailed description of oddments is given as an aid to the spinner.

NECK WOOL. This wool can be likened to a collar around the sheep's neck. It lies between the shoulder wools at the head of a fleece when it is spread out intact on the floor. On a fully-grown fleece there is about 5 oz of neck wool—it is fine and "flannel" soft with a shade or colour of its own. It can be combed out to remove "moit" or vegetable matter, and washed to remove dust or dirt. After washing it should be dried and oiled slightly before spinning.

Spun on its own it will produce a fine soft yarn, and blended with body wool it will give a soft handle or feel to the finished yarn. It dyes well, giving soft pastel shades. It is generally as long as body wool, well grown and even in fibre content, having sound tensile properties and evenness of fibre diameter or count.

BELLY WOOL. This wool is practically always absent from the body wool as the shearer takes it off first and throws it aside to be binned separately. As stated earlier, it can look dirty, grimy and short and will contain some staining when removed from male sheep. However, the good and super grades of belly wool can be long and clean giving a sound, curly and springy fibre which will give "pile" and springiness to a yarn spun from it. Belly wool is fairly hard to spin in the natural greasy state but when washed, dried, oiled and combed it will soften and spin, especially when blended with body wool. Belly wool will dye well—giving varying shades because of its often lustrous character.

LEG WOOL—(POINTS AND PIECES). Commonly called pieces, they come in firsts and seconds, the first pieces being the longer and heavier-conditioned and discoloured wools skirted from the main fleece to leave a uniform parcel of body wool. The second pieces are the wools of short content—considerably shorter than the firsts and more heavy in condition and discoloration. Their length does not exceed more than 2 in. and because of this they are more suitable for blending with longer fibres. They wash well and can be used to create the tufty woollen type yarns of the homespun effect. All pieces are likely to contain some hair or short white kemps—these fibres do not take dye in the same way as pure wool but they create some interesting shades and effects in the yarns produced containing them. (The tweeds of Scotland and the Border countries and many of the wellknown tweeds of England contain piece wools from the various breeds in the British Isles which are inclined to have hairy fibres in their fleeces.)

SOME SUGGESTIONS FOR USING POORER TYPES OF WOOLS

MAKING AN EIDERDOWN OR A SLEEPING-BAG.

The standard size for a single bed eiderdown is 4 ft by 5 ft (approx.).

The standard size for a double bed eiderdown is 5 ft by 6 ft (approx.).

The sizes for a sleeping-bag are as follows:
  Standard: 75″ x 30″ x 24″ (these being the length x width at shoulders x width at bottom).
  Large OS size: 80″ x 30″ x 24″.
  Side-zip: 30 in.
  Approx. weight: 4 lb 6 oz – 4 lb 8 oz.

  Materials: Openwork medical gauze or butter muslin 2 pieces required, 4ft 4 in. by 5 ft 4 in. clean washed wool (allow 1½ lb for a single bed eiderdown) material for outer cover.

TO MAKE THE INNER WOOLLY SECTION. With the fingers tease the wool, fluffing it so that there are no hard lumps (carders are not necessary). On to each piece of the 4 ft 4 in. by 5 ft 4 in. gauze material sew the wool in long tacking threads. Now place the two woolly sides of the gauze together like the filling of a sandwich. Stitch the 4 sides together. Remember that too much wool makes the eiderdown too heavy, too little does not supply sufficient warmth.

The purpose of sewing-in the wool is to prevent it from shifting and becoming bulky and lumpy. This is an important factor when laundering both eiderdowns and sleeping-bags. They can stand light laundering and spin drying, and be exposed to sunshine drying, and the finished product is as good as new, even after many, many washings.

To cover your wool eiderdown, obey the following instructions. Material for covering eiderdown and sleeping-bag must be light and closely woven, with a smooth finish such as a down proof sateen or japara, or fine close cotton with a mercerised finish. At least one side of an eiderdown should be non-slippery.

Cut material to exact width and length plus 1½ in. seam allowance. Depending on the width of your material, join it or not, as required. In most cases some joins are necessary, but a 48 in. material would be wide enough for a single-bed eiderdown. If joining, do so at the sides, not in the centre panel, and the seams should coincide with lines of quilting. If the pattern is striped or in a large floral design it should be centred carefully in the panel. Sew material on three sides like a pillow-case and slip inside the prepared wool and muslin. Sew up the fourth side. Finish with quilting. If a small frill is planned as trimming on the edges, this must be tacked into the seam before being stitched.

A sleeping-bag is covered in a similar manner, but remember to machine-in a zip fastener.

Above: Knot stitch being worked in unspun fleece wool on a canvas backing. Note the trammed canvas in wool to make extra thickness. *(By courtesy Alice McFarlane.)*

WOOL ON CANVAS BACKING

Thick homespun used single, doubled or trebled, carpet wool in various thicknesses and colours, machine-carded wool tops (sometimes called rovings) can be embroidered or knotted on very open canvas to make a variety of useful articles for the home such as fire screens, floor rugs, chair coverings, stool tops, shopping baskets etc.

In all canvas work the whole of the ground fabric is to be covered so it is very important to select the right mesh canvas and the corresponding right thickness of wool yarn that will make the best filling.

Canvasses can be bought with the design already printed and trammed, i.e. a lengthwise stitch of an appropriate colour has been made over each group of canvas threads to be covered. The design and colour scheme are thus clearly indicated and in addition the extra covering or padding thread forms a thicker backing. It is understandable that trammed canvasses will be more expensive and sooner or later any needlewoman will prefer to design her own. The materials chosen should look and wear well, they should be suitable to the purpose for which the work will be used, and they should be pleasant to work with.

Sample the stitches first on a small corner of the canvas to see which yarn and which stitch will cover the canvas best.

The following have been tried out successfully:

THE MAKING OF A WOOL MAT IN PILE RUG STITCH

MATERIALS REQUIRED: Coarse canvas the size of the finished mat plus 2 in. extra on the 4 sides. Thick homespun wool or long-staple fleece wool washed but kept in its staple bundles. Crochet hook or rug hook with latchet.

METHOD: Cut the spun wool into equal lengths (approx. 3 in.–4 in.). This is best done by winding the wool around a smooth, even board, then cutting down one edge. Take a single piece of wool and double it in half. With a crochet hook draw the loop through two holes, passing under one cross thread. Now pass the two ends of thread through the loop and draw it up tightly, keeping the ends even. The tighter this is drawn up the more secure will the wool be fastened to the canvas. Put the threads closely together if a very thick mat is desired, and use wool of such a thickness that it will fill each space. A blending of spun wool and unspun fleece wool makes an interesting texture. Though the mat is flat on the underside it wears better if lined—hessian makes a good lining.

Below: Heather Mill working a hooked floor rug on canvas using her own 2-ply spun wool.

29

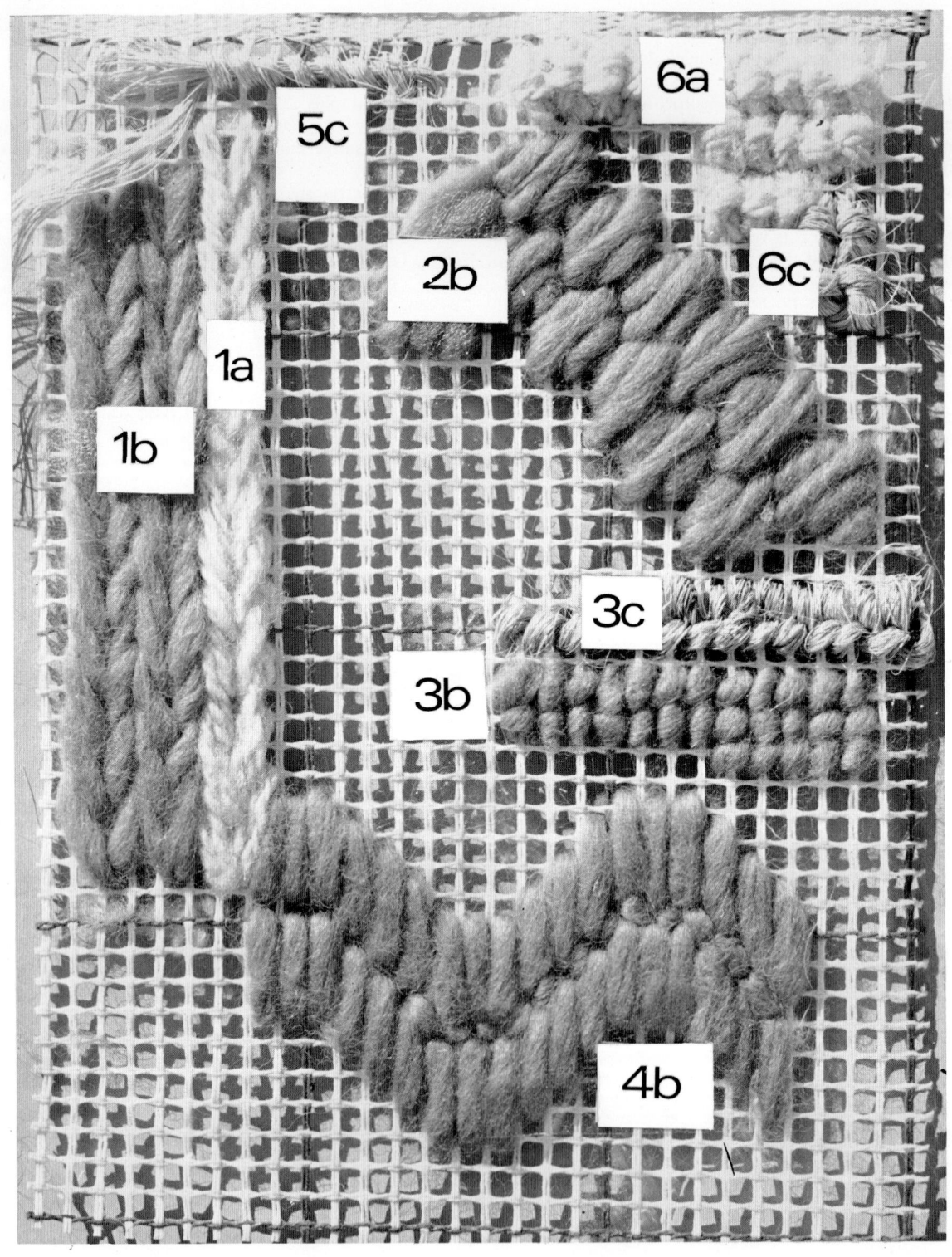

STITCHES FOR CANVAS WORK. The materials used on this sample are:
(a) Thick wool.   (b) Wool tops.   (c) Flax.
   The stitches shown are numbered for identification and fully described on the opposite page.

30

STITCHES FOR CANVAS WORK

1. *Fern stitch.* Work from bottom upward with very thick thread. Come up at A, pass up over two holes with a slanting stitch to B. Working horizontally from right to left pass under one hole to C. Another slanting stitch from C back over two holes to A—on the wrong side pass under the thick thread at A and bring the needle up to a new hole just above A. Repeat as required.

2. *Milanese stitch or diagonal satin.* Work from left to right. On the wide-holed canvas, slope the satin stitch over one hole, then two, then three, back to two, and one. This is a useful stitch for colour shading and can be massed as triangles also in colour.

3. *Tent stitch or petit point or half cross.* A versatile stitch used effectively in the finest tapestry as well as in the coarsest canvas. A diagonal stitch is made from left up to right, crossing over two strands of canvas each way. The needle is passed vertically downward beneath the canvas between each stitch.

4. *Hungarian stitch* (and its variations). A stitch worked in vertical lines, one encroaching upon the other so as to cover the canvas completely. The sampler shows a lined Hungarian stitch to add extra thickness.

   (a) A vertical stitch crosses two threads of canvas, each stitch being one strand apart. The second stitch begins opposite the middle of the first one; this gives an interesting stippled effect.

   (b) Alternate long and short stitches are used, the first stitch passing over two strands of canvas and the second over one strand.

5. *The Gobelin stitch.* The one shown here is a straight vertical one, passing over two parallel threads of canvas. It gives a corded surface particularly when trammed with the extra thread. Straight Gobelin stitch can be done in two ways.

   Upper: The stitch is made over trammed ground.
   Lower: The ground is left untrammed.

6. *Knot Barred cross stitch.* (Refer page 28.) Start from left, cross diagonally over three (count the hole you bring the needle up through, over one complete hole, and number three hole is the one the needle passes down into). Come back horizontally under one, cross over three, and to form the bar come up the middle hole and straight across. Repeat. This stitch, like number 3 on the sampler, is shown in flax as well as in wool.

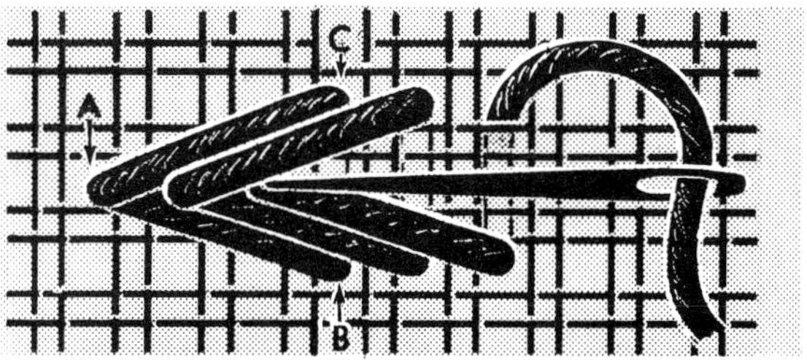

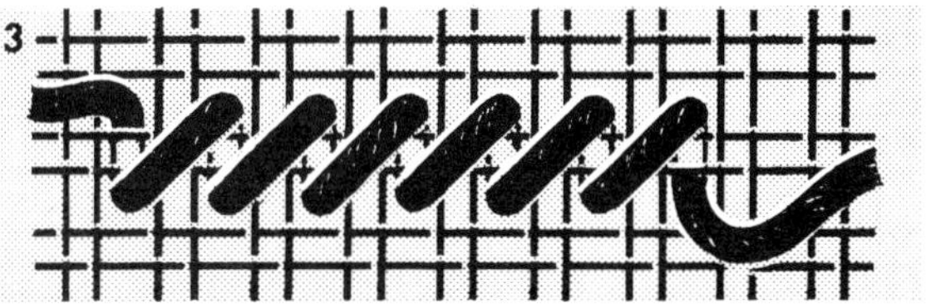

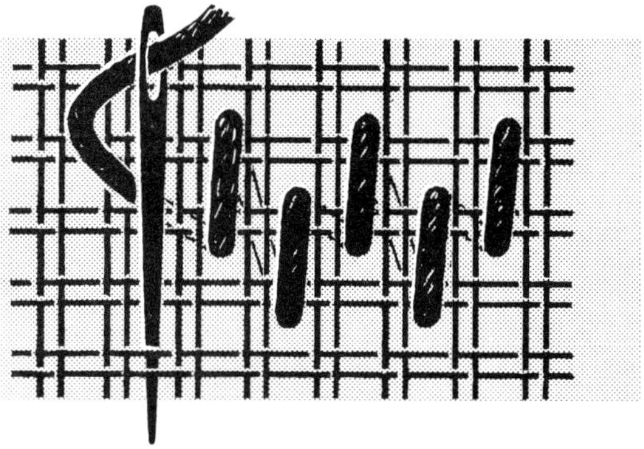

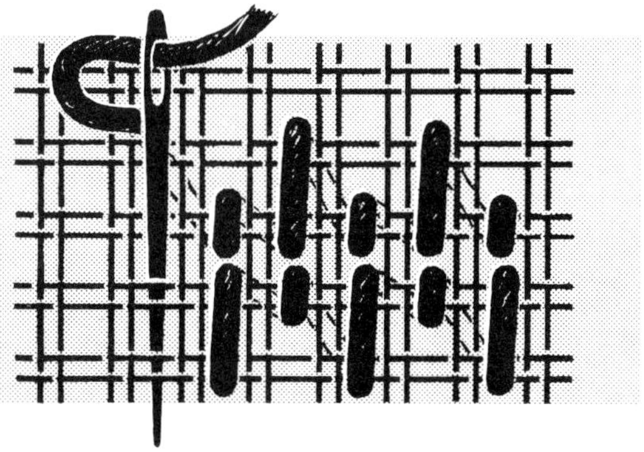

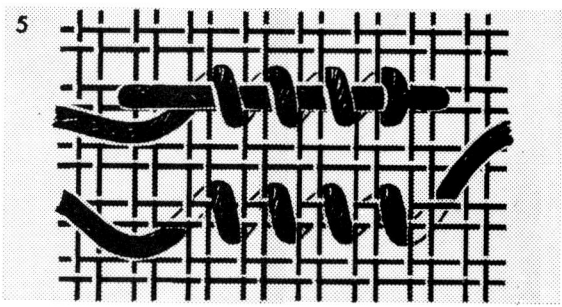

Woven floor rug—white and grey rolags of carded fleece wool forming an irregular pattern. Full directions for weaving will be found on the opposite page.

WOVEN FLOOR RUG IN WHITE AND GREY FLEECE WOOL

WARP: Linen flax seaming twine.

WEFT: Carded white and grey fleece wool.

WARP ENDS: 170 for finished width of 45 in.

ENDS TO THE INCH: 4.

REED: 8.

DENTING: 1 full, 1 empty.

FINISHED LENGTH: 80 in.

THREADING: Tabby.

TREADLING: 1, 2.

WEAVING PLAN:

    a. Leave 6 in. for fringe if fringe is desired.

or b. Weave 1 in. with flax seaming twine.

    c. Weave ¾ in. of thick homespun in grey and white speckled mixture.

    d. Weave ¾ in. with flax seaming twine.

    (b, c and d make a firm attractive edging which can be bound at b with standard carpet edging and folded back and stitched. This avoids having a knotted fringe which tends to fray at the ends after hard wear.)

    e. The main texture—Shed 1 lay in lightly twisted rolags of the white and grey carded wool building up a pattern. Beat tightly. Shed 2. Beat again before laying in another row. Repeat for 80 in.

    f. Weave a border to correspond with b, c, d.

VARIATIONS WOVEN ON THE SAME SETTING

    1. A shaggy rug—for directions see weaving an Invalid's Hospital Underblanket (page 39). For the floor rug, wash the fleece wool first, keeping it in staple form as much as possible.

    2. Weave 2 rows of homespun or carpet wool doubled between each row of rolags.

Details of a firm edging for a floor rug.

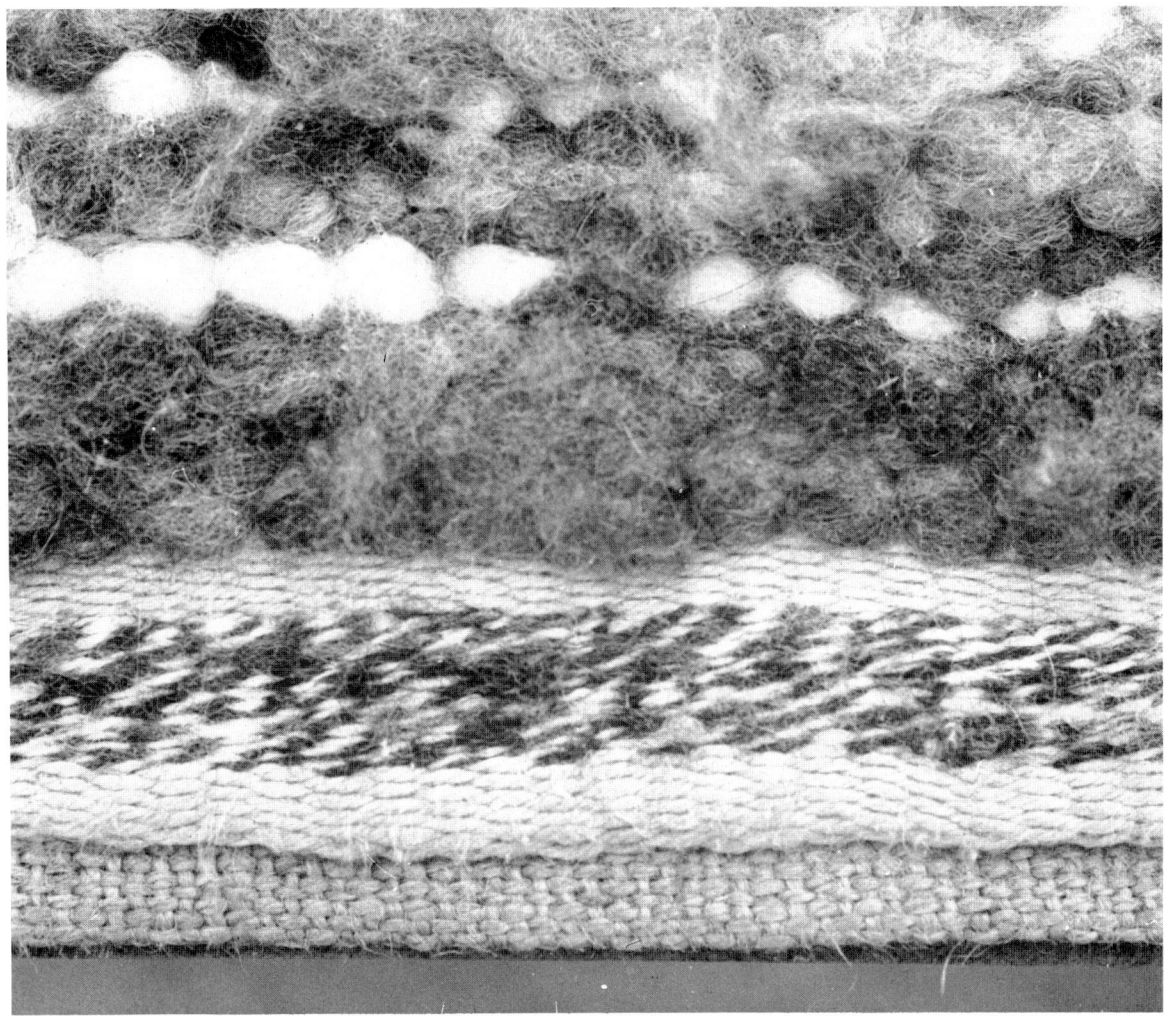

HOW TO PLAN TAPESTRY

1. Decide on the size measurements and note these on the sketch plan. Calculate the warp width and the woven length allowing for shrinkage and warp take-up.

2. Plan the colour scheme, the shading proportions, and the position of the definite shapes. Though it is possible to develop the free-merging colours on the loom itself by referring only to the small sketch plan, it is advisable to have a more detailed enlargement for the regular areas.

3. Make an enlarged cartoon of the regular shapes and pin these under the warp threads. This can roll along with the warp as the tapestry progresses.

4. To keep the width even and to prevent the tapestry "drawing it", weave with the temple or stretcher ½ in. below the working area. Alternatively, measure the width inch by inch.

5. When weaving definite shapes there is a tendency to build them up much higher than the background. Do this if necessary for a 1 in. to 1½ in., but as the background is brought up to the same height then use the beater to check the straight line of the woven width.

A FOUR-STRANDED PLAIT: (To edge all four sides of a tapestry). If the background colour is used for the plait and sewn along the four edges the plaiting gives a finished framed appearance to the tapestry, combining the colour scheme with a neat finish to the woven side edges.

TO MAKE THE FOUR-STRAND PLAIT. Start by carrying the left outside strand over the strand next to it, then the outside right strand should be carried under the strand next to it. The two outside strands are now in the middle; cross them and repeat the three steps outlined. Leave sufficient thread at the start and the finish of the plait to make tassels at all four corners, if desired.

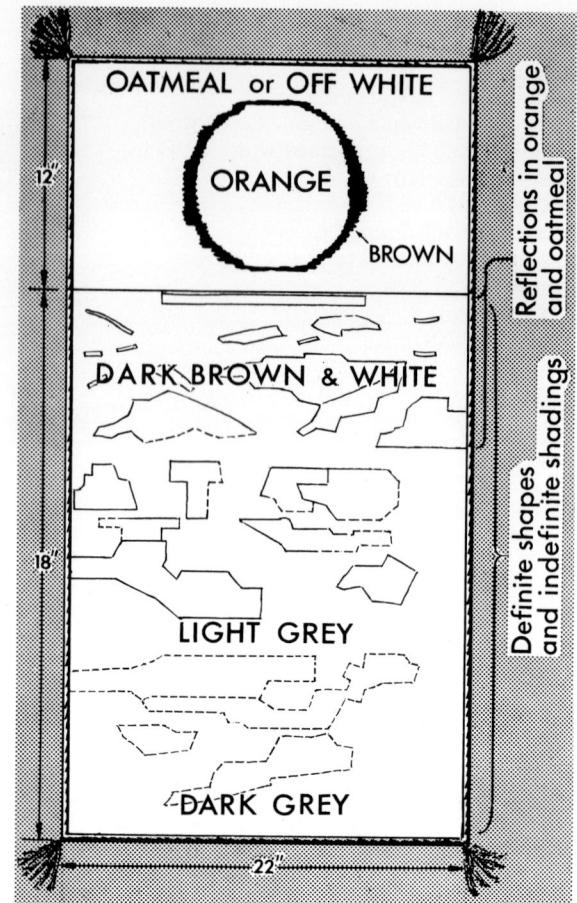

"Sun and Strata"—details of the strata.

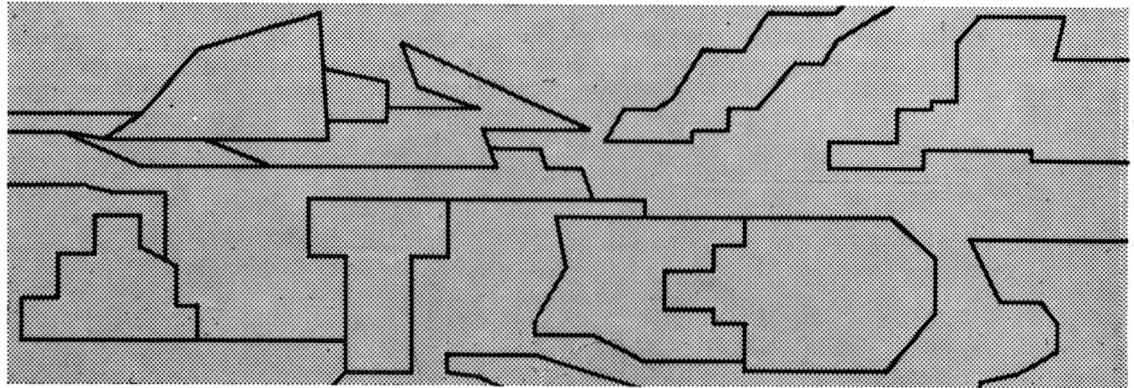

"Sun and Strata"—a woven tapestry showing a range of natural wools in grey, white and plant dyed colours. This tapestry has a four-stranded plait edging.

35

WOVEN TAPESTRY ON THE LOOM USING HOMESPUN WOOL

WARP: Linen flax seaming twine.
WEFT: Homespun wool.
WARP ENDS: 136 for 22 in. finished width.
ENDS TO THE INCH: 6.
REED: 10.
DENTING: 2 full, 1 empty.

THREADING: Tabby.
TREADLING: 1, 2   Table looms   .. 1 and 3, 2 and 4.
FINISHED LENGTH: 40 in.

N.B. This is a flat weave perfected by the Navajo Indians who used strong well-twisted homespun wool for the warp threads and the weft was wool of softer, thicker texture. Warp set at 6–8 ends per inch and a firm heavy beater packed down the weft.

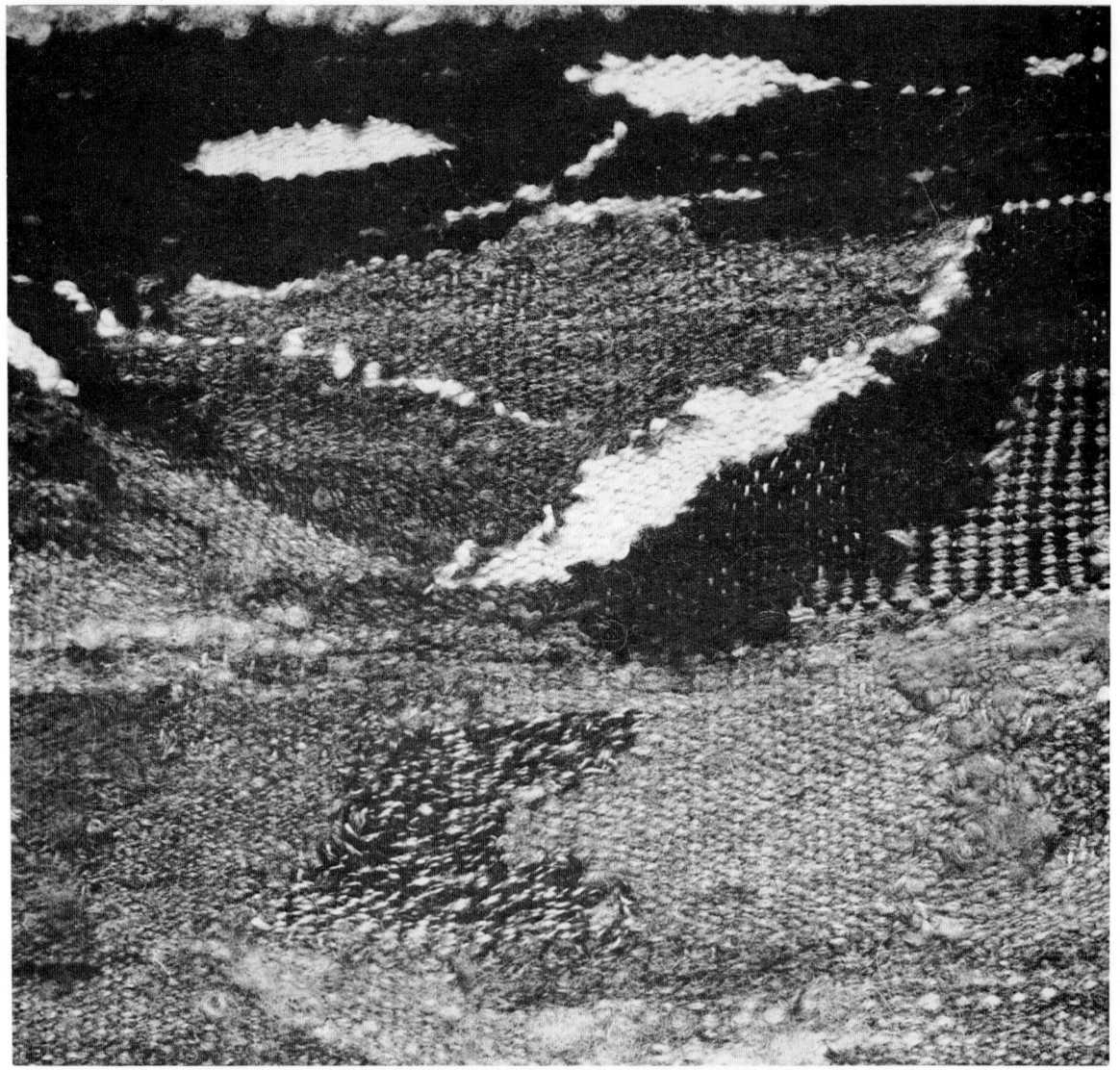

An enlarged section of the "Sun and Strata" woven tapestry.

FINISHING THE EDGES OF A WOVEN TAPESTRY OR A FLOOR RUG

The New Zealand Maori in their taaniko weaving had a casting-off technique that can be adapted to make a firm, twisted edging with the warp ends. After finger-weaving the edge the warp ends lie parallel on the underside of the woven fabric ready to be darned in.

This twisted edging makes a strong finish to a floor rug or, when a hem is not required, to edge a table mat or the top of a bag.

Have the right side of the weaving uppermost and the cut warp ends hanging at the top. Start from the left-hand side. This edging is worked with 2 threads up, 2 threads down.

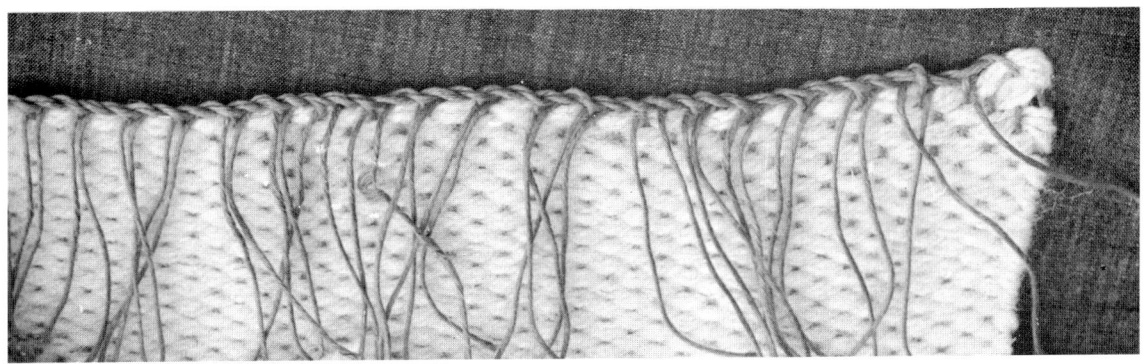

The taaniko edging finished and showing the warp ends (on the wrong side) ready to be darned in.

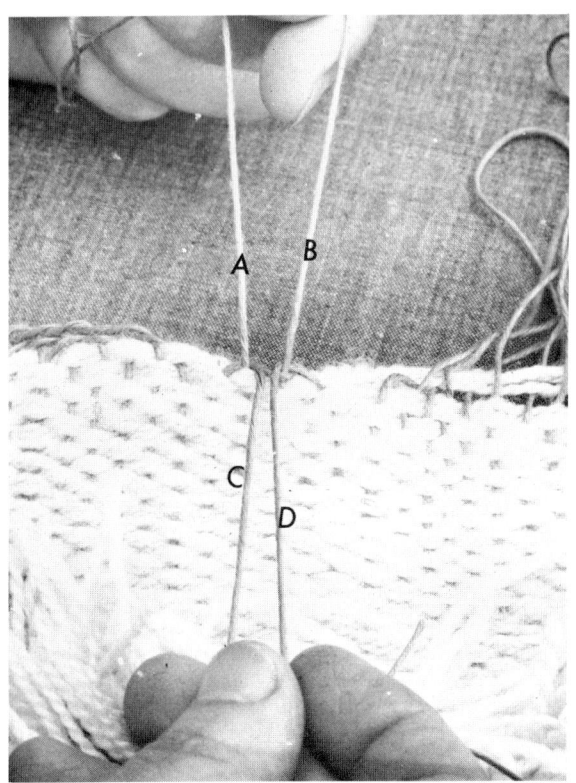

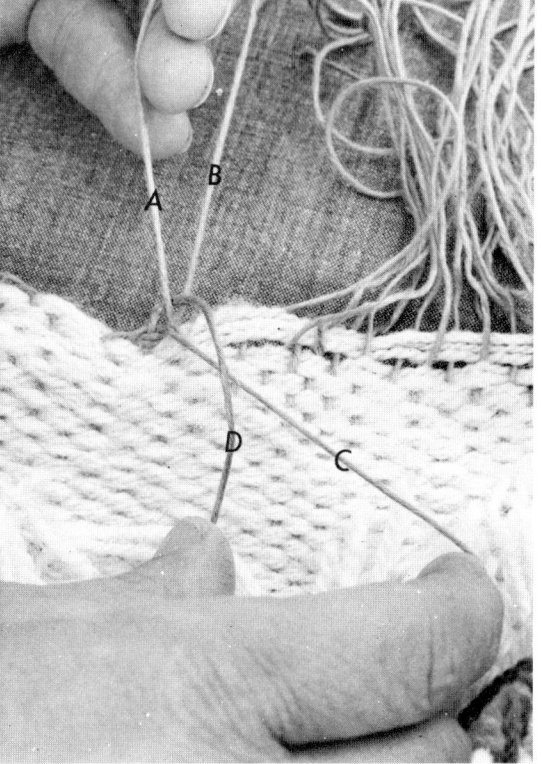

Taaniko edging—two threads up.

Step 1   —two threads down.

Step 2   —cross D over C.

Step 3   —B thread bend back to the wrong
side.
A thread still in original position.
C and D still crossed.

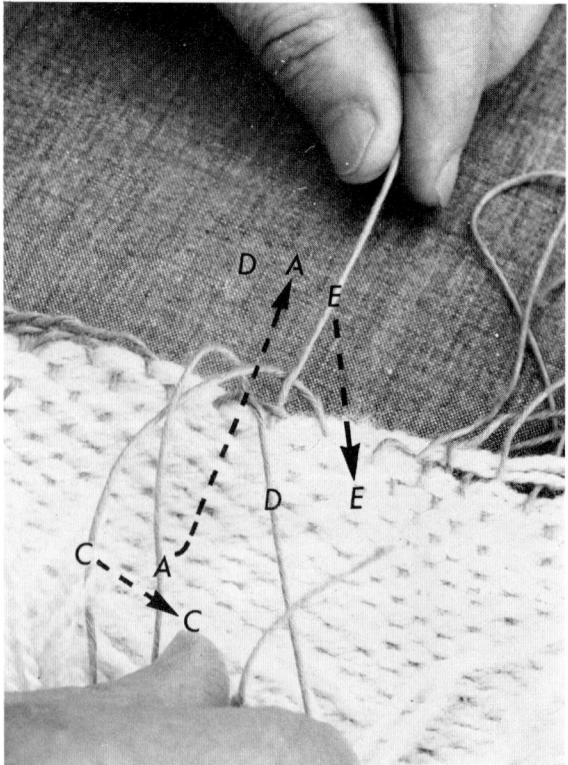

Step 4   —A thread now bends down between
C and D.

Step 5   —D bends up to form a new "up"
thread on the left-hand side.
C passes over A in its new position
and becomes the "down" thread
on the left-hand side.
A brings in a new thread "E"
passing under it and swinging up
to make the second "up" thread.
E falls down to the second "down"
thread on the right-hand side.
Once again there are two "up"
and two "down". With practice
a rhythm of movement develops
that helps to keep the edge even.

PLANNING AND WEAVING SEVERAL ITEMS ON THE SAME WARP

(A Cushion, A Bag, An Invalid's Hospital Underblanket)

WARP: White carpet wool.
WEFT: Homespun carpet and/or fleece wool unspun.
WARP ENDS: 264 for finished width of 22 in.
ENDS PER INCH: 12.
REED: 12.
DENTING: 1 per dent.
FINISHED LENGTH: Cushion 22 in., bag 32 in., hospital underblanket 36 in.
WARP LENGTH: 4½ yards.
THREADING: Tabby.
WEAVING PLAN:

Cushion: Plan the weft for rows of carded fleece wool in natural wools, plant-dyed colours, and chemical-dyed colours. Shafts 1 and 2 . . . fleece wool carded in long thin rolags the thickness of the little finger. 2 shots of tabby, i.e. 1 and 3 and 2 and 4. Shafts 3 and 4 . . . fleece wool as before. 2 shots of tabby.

Bag: Can be woven as for cushion, in different colour combinations, and/or all white homespun woven with a twill border. Twill combination on this threading is:

A combination is 1 and 2 shafts lifted
B combination is 2 and 3 shafts lifted
C combination is 3 and 4 shafts lifted
D combination is 4 and 1 shafts lifted

and/or the twill border in carded fleece wool and the rest plain homespun. Weave 2 in. of tabby, 3 in. border of twill, 1 in. tabby, 1½ in. twill, 1 in. tabby, ¾ in. twill. This makes 10¼ in. border.

Weave 11½ in. of all tabby then repeat the 10¼ in. border. The total for the bag should add to 32 in. Bag handles can be woven on the inkle loom (as shown in *Spin Your Own Wool*) or tightly twist or plait 6 thicknesses of homespun wool.

The Invalid's Hospital Underblanket. These have been proved invaluable for patients confined to bed for some length of time but they must be woven with fleece wool unwashed, so that the lanolin grease is retained. Select a really greasy fleece of soft quality and discard any dirty ends. Neck wools are particularly suitable for this.

WEAVING PLAN: Weave 6 rows of tabby in carpet wool. Next row: on a closed shed, take a staple of the greasy fleece wool *no thicker than ¼ in.* and knot it around 2 warp threads as shown in *Spin Your Own Wool*, page 44, Fig. 23. Continue right across the warp. Repeat 6 rows of tabby followed by a row of knotted fleece until the 36 in. is completed.

N.B. This weaving plan used with non-greasy fleece makes a delightful shaggy floor rug in either all-white wool, or white and natural blends, or plant-dyed wools and natural fleece. Smaller versions in the same technique make pet blankets for wicker baskets. A strip folded over and sewn on two sides like a pillowslip makes an excellent foot-warmer for passengers in a car to slip their feet into for protection from draughts —or for fireside use at home.

To Make up the Knitting Bag. Materials required: The woven length. Lining material and tailor's canvas for stiffening if necessary. A 16 in. zip. Handles made of twisted rug wool.

To make: Cut out shapes for bag and gussets from plan ½ in. larger. With the zigzag stitch on your sewing machine zigzag around all cut edges to prevent fraying. If using tailor's canvas this could be zigzagged in place with the shapes of the woven material. When covering gussets leave material open across the short end. Cut a 16-inch slit down centre of gusset strip and tack zip behind this. Make tiny diagonal slits at each end so that ¼ in. can be turned in down sides. Machine or back stitch zip in place.

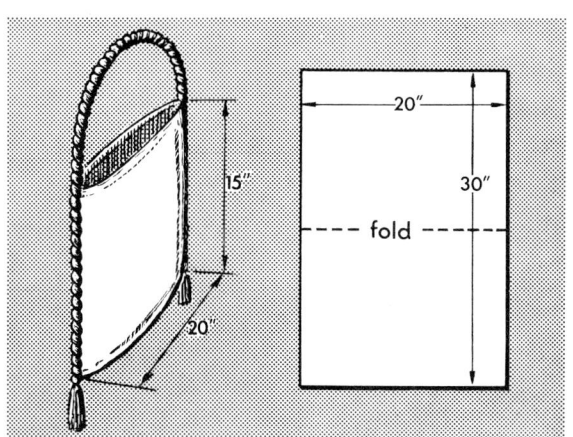

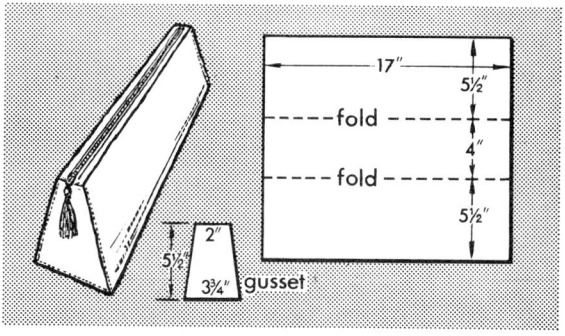

Now cut lining ½ in. larger than required, pin into position and slip-stitch down the two sides but leave top and bottom open.

Fold bag on dotted lines and press under a damp cloth.

Place gussets right-side downward at each end of gusset strips as in diagram, and machine across the ends close to the ends of canvas. It is important that strips should measure same as width of bag. Turn back gussets and press. Find centre of zip and centre of bag; place raw edges of strips behind front edge of bag and pin. Pin opposite edge to back of bag, and stitch across firmly. Undo zip and turn inside out. Bring up lining to cover raw edges and slip-stitch. Now fold down gussets and over-sew to sides of bag. Make a tab or tassel and stitch to end of zip.

A toy in brightly coloured thick homespun wools.

A WOOLLY TOY IN HOMESPUN WOOLS: *MR AND MRS OCTOPUS*

Two skeins are required. Wind them for length either on a skeiner or around the back of a chair.

To form a head for the octopus, tie the skein tightly at one end, and about 3 inches down tie again to form the neck. The thickness of the two skeins should form a roundish head. At the other end of the double skeins cut through, leaving loose threads. Divide these loose ends into 8 parts. Plait them and tie securely—they form the long tentacles of the octopus. Mrs Octopus could have her tentacles tied with pretty coloured bows.

Make an interesting face, working the eyes, nose and mouth in satin stitch of a bright contrasting-colour wool. It is not wise to use a button or a bead for the face if the toy is for a small child, as they soon pull apart and can be easily swallowed.

Crochet a hat in single and double crochet—trim with flowers using lazy-daisy stitch for Mrs Octopus; make Mr Octopus a very colourful tie.

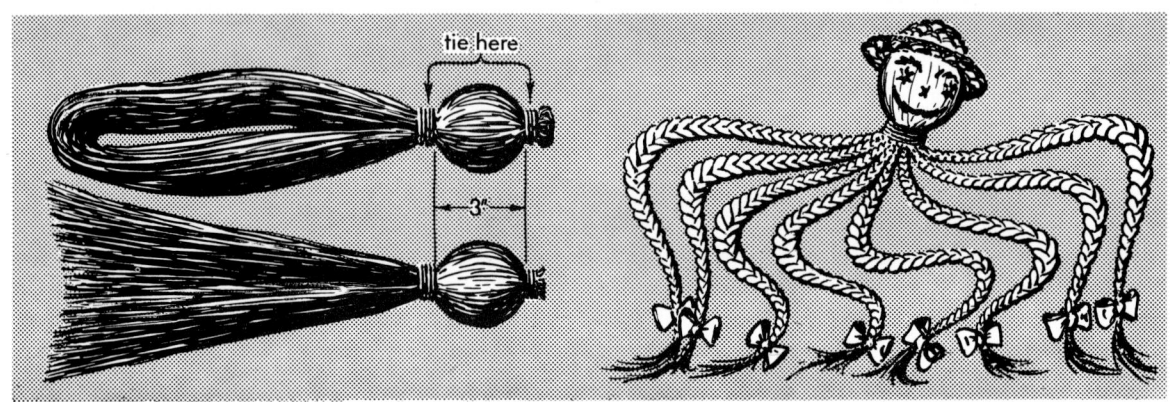

Chapter 5

FLAX AND ITS THREADS

FLAX in all its different forms should not be overlooked by spinners and weavers. There are many varieties, yielding fibres of differing characters.

The imported Irish flax-linen can feel as soft as silk and be bleached white or left natural. It comes in the form of tops, long continuous slivers like our wool tops—or in cut form in 6 in. bundles. Spin it as you do wool or cotton, feeding it into the spindle by hand.

However, this section of the book is principally concerned with *Phormium tenax*, the flax indigenous to New Zealand. Certain varieties of this, too, can be threshed as soft and fine as silk, as evidenced in many ancient Maori garments such as the cloak of a high-ranking chief.

Phormium tenax belongs to the lily family, there being two, if not more, main distinct varieties differing from each other in the colour of their flowers, the one being red and the other yellow. The plant itself has a fanlike appearance, the leaves springing from the root stock in the form of a fan and growing to a height of 8 ft to 10 ft. Each leaf is folded on itself along the midrib with the upper surface innermost, while on the lower or outermost surface the midrib forms a sharp keel along the back of the leaf.

Leaves in each group of fans are arranged in two sets facing each other, one on either side of the growing point, the thickened and roughly v-shaped base of each enclosing a younger one in its fold. When cutting flax leaves yourself, leave this young leaf undamaged so as to protect the plant, but cut on either side leaves of a year to 18-months' growth and those that are beginning to split at the end and curl over from the centre midrib.

As *Phormium tenax* does not produce a true strain from seed, propagation of the desired type is obtained by splitting the parent bush into a number of fans which are then replanted in a suitable manner.

The Flax Plant used for nature stitchery.
Spun flax for the outside edging, flax pods split and the tips couched in place to represent the petals of a flower.
For the centre—coils of machinespun thread and secured with P.V.A. 85 glue. Flax seeds also glued on plus a few short cut flax fibres sprinkled over to soften the effect.

The fibres lie longitudinally in the leaf surrounded by a cuticle or epidermis of a glutinous and chlorophyllic nature and it is this that presents the greatest obstacle in cleaning the fibre. The plant contains 14 per cent of fibre in its leaves in comparison with $2\frac{1}{2}$ per cent to $3\frac{1}{2}$ per cent for manila fibre and 3.4 per cent for sisal fibre. Thus *P. tenax* has the highest yield of fibre for any of the known fibre plants. Research and progress have led to this remarkable yield, and one respects more and more the work of the early Maoris who were able to use only a quarter of each leaf, laboriously scraped with sharp shells on flat rocks for the ropemaking export industry of the 19th and early 20th century.

Nowadays the long fibre is valuable for many industrial purposes which include fibre for cordages, lashings, baling twine, plasterers' tow, upholsterers' tow, matting, and woolpacks. For floor-covering manufacture the fibres are blended with sisal, jute, and viscose rayon and dyed in various colours with these fibres.

Hanks of stripped washed flax hang on fences in the paddocks to dry and bleach in the sunshine, a process which takes from two to three weeks, then back to the

mill for the scutching, drawing out and combing, blending, dyeing, spinning, weaving, and finishings.

The milling process in industry is a help to the craftsman who wishes to examine all possibilities of textile technology for his own expression. By handling these fibres and learning their potentials a wide range of ideas unfolds—wool can be spun with flax, also wool with sisal, and, as another combination, substitute raw cotton for the wool.

Weaving and embroidering, too, use these fibres, spun or unspun, in endless combinations.

HOW TO SPIN FLAX

Fine threshed flax, almost as fine as silk, presents no spinning problem—treat it like wool or cotton. But the longer fibres and coarser textures are more difficult to deal with unless they are dampened and the spinner has her fingers slightly wet. The spun flax looks like fluffy string.

When spinning with tow, i.e. what is left after the combing process, draw out the tow from the top, making a long sliver, and then put in the twist to form

a yarn. Tow cannot be handled too much, otherwise it falls apart. Test the strength of your twisted yarn to make sure you have sufficient twists. Aim to have irregularities, otherwise it may look like mill-spun string. Too few twists make a weak thread—too many make a hard twisted wrinkly coil and not a manageable thread. Watch always for the angle of your twists to keep them regular and consistent.

As with wool spinning, proper co-ordination between drafting with the hands and treadling with the feet will determine the angle of the twist. A skilful spinner will make variations by design, not by accident.

To join, lap untwisted flax to untwisted—unlike wool it does not join readily to an already-twisted thread. A little extra wetting may help in joining; otherwise most of the spinning techniques in wool spinning apply to flax.

The flax threads illustrated below show, on the left, actual-size threads and, on the right, the same threads enlarged so that the characteristics are more clearly seen.

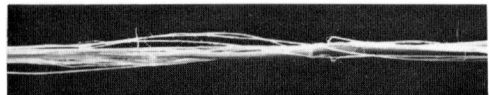 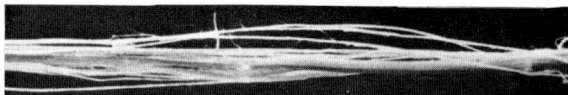

1. *Phormium tenax* roughly threshed. The coarse flax thread retains some of the cuticle. This adds to the colour of the fibre.

 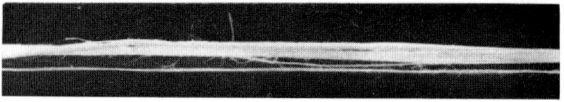

2. *Phormium tenax*, a finer threshing. This is all one colour and is softer to handle than the roughly-threshed thread.

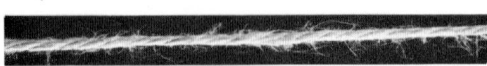 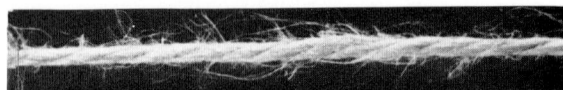

3. Machinespun linen flax, seaming twine—2 twist No. 206. The double twist can be clearly seen in the enlarged photo.

 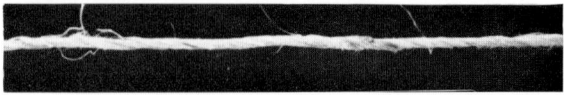

4. Handspun *Phormium tenax*—fine thread.

 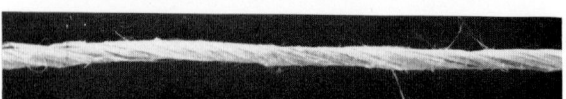

5. Handspun *Phormium tenax*—thick thread.

6. Handspun *Phormium tenax* from cut lengths of 10 in. – 12 in. and therefore jagged in appearance.

 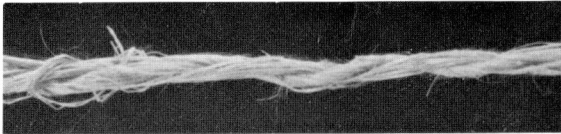

7. Handspun *Phormium tenax* in a 2-ply uneven textured twisting.

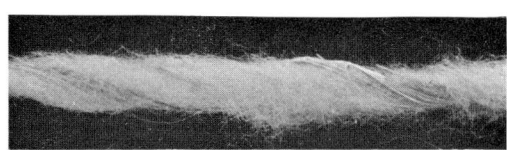 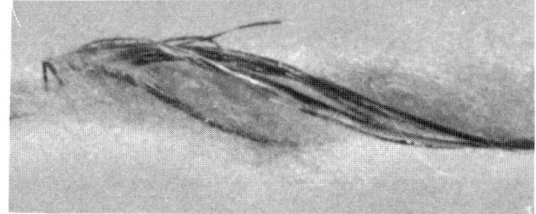

8. Wool and flax spun together. The flax shows dark in the photograph—a straight jagged fibre against a fluffy one.

 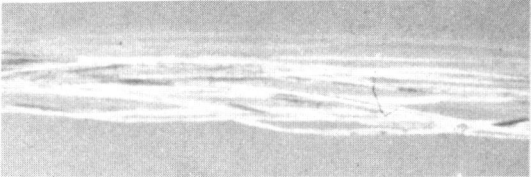

9. Sisal strands. As can be seen, they are much whiter in appearance than the flax fibre.

10. Sisal and wool spun together. The enlargement shows the fluffy wool and the straight loop of sisal.

EMBROIDERY WEAVING is a term to describe ornamenting a fabric while it is still on the loom being woven. It is known also as *free weaving* since the pattern is controlled by the weaver and not by the threading and treadling of the loom. Its other names are *finger weaving* or *laid-in weaving*, the work being done mostly by the fingers in preference to shuttles; the newest of all these terms is *art weaving*, so called because often a sketch or design is drawn first.

The five samples shown on the following pages worked with unspun flax on a linen warp are favourite old techniques that present a new appearance when woven with coarser threads.

All are examples of openwork weave, and there are many more that are equally interesting with the heavier threads.

WARP FOR THESE EXPERIMENTS: Hayes linen thread No. 18, 3 cord.

NUMBER OF WARP THREADS: 120 for a 6 in. width.

REED: No. 10.

DENTING: 2 per dent.

THREADING: Tabby.

If the weaver has a small Swedish embroidery shuttle it can be used to put through each twist as it is made and thus carry the weft thread across.

N.B. Because of the slippery nature of the linen warp used for the sample, a line of hemstitching was worked before starting the leno twist. This kept the flax strands in place on the plain weave and showed up the twists more distinctly. It is not always necessary to do this hemstitching, indeed it often spoils the openwork appearance.

LENO LACE WOVEN ON A LOOM USING THRESHED FLAX ON A LINEN WARP

Leno is an example of openwork formed by twisting warp threads in certain combinations. The twist made on a closed shed is more distinct than on an open shed. Leno is a particularly adaptable openwork technique, not only looking attractive on very fine linen where it really has a lacy appearance, but also on bolder thicker materials where it still gives a softened look, showing up the textures in light and shadow of the warp and weft threads.

Any combinations of twisted threads can be used—3 over 3, 2 over 2, 1 over 1—and the twists do not necessarily have to extend right across a warp. Geometric blocks of twists can form a pattern, or a twist can be the effect texture between straight threads, e.g. a 2 over 2 twist, then 4 straight threads, and repeat this across the entire warp.

HOW TO MAKE THE TWIST. 3 over 3 leno looks more effective on the linen warp in this sample. Counting from the right-hand side hold the first 3 warp threads with the left-hand fingers while picking up threads 4, 5 and 6 with the right-hand fingers. Pull 4, 5 and 6 to the right under 1, 2 and 3 and twist them as a group up over the first group. With a ruler or similar thin stick, slide these twisted threads on to the stick so as to hold the twist. Work right across the warp, twisting 3 over 3 in groups and sliding them on to the ruler. Now turn the ruler on its side, thus forming a small shed, and with the shuttle pass the weft thread through the opening from right to left. Return the shuttle from left to right on the plain weave shed.

Leno twist in groups of six twisted warp threads.

44

Brooks Bouquet in groups of 12 threads.

BROOKS BOUQUET

This is a lovely-sounding name for a simple technique of wrapping threads around a group of warp ends. Used traditionally on fine weave and fine threads, Brooks Bouquet deserved its name for its beautiful small open spaces. It is included here because it combines very well with leno in creative stitchery and weaving together.

Directions. Groupings can be bold on this linen warp and the flax weft. For wrapping, work with your fingers or use a short shuttle. As for leno, keep the shed closed and work from right to left.

Take 6 warp ends, bring the wrapping threads from under, pass them around the first 6 warp ends, continue back under the same group but go under the next 6 warp ends. Bring the wrapping threads up from under, pass them around the second group of 6 warp ends, down and behind the second group and add 6 more warp threads.

The wrap stitch includes the selvedge so should not be pulled too tightly, and beating will depend on the desired effect and the materials used.

SPANISH LACE

SPANISH LACE. This version of openwork weave has many possibilities for table runners, window blinds, room dividers, shopping bags, etc. Whereas leno and Brooks Bouquet were made on a closed shed, Spanish lace is worked on the tabby shafts in groups of 10 warp ends (if your warp ends are not equally divisible by 10 include the extra threads equally on the selvedge groups).

Treadle shafts 1 and 3, pass shuttle under 10 threads from right-hand side.

Treadle shafts 2 and 4, and return shuttle under 10 threads from left to right.

Treadle 1 and 3, pass shuttle under 10 threads from right to left. Push the flax down slightly between the two threads, one ending this group and the first of the next group of 10, to make a rounded shape. Do not beat.

Treadle 2 and 4, pass shuttle under next 10 threads from right to left.

Treadle 1 and 3, pass shuttle under 10 threads from left to right.

Treadle 2 and 4, pass shuttle under 10 threads from right to left. Push the flax down as before to make the rounded shape. Do not beat.

Repeat right across the warp.

Weave 2 rows of tabby or shafts 1 and 2, then shafts 3 and 4 with the flax. Make another line of Spanish lace.

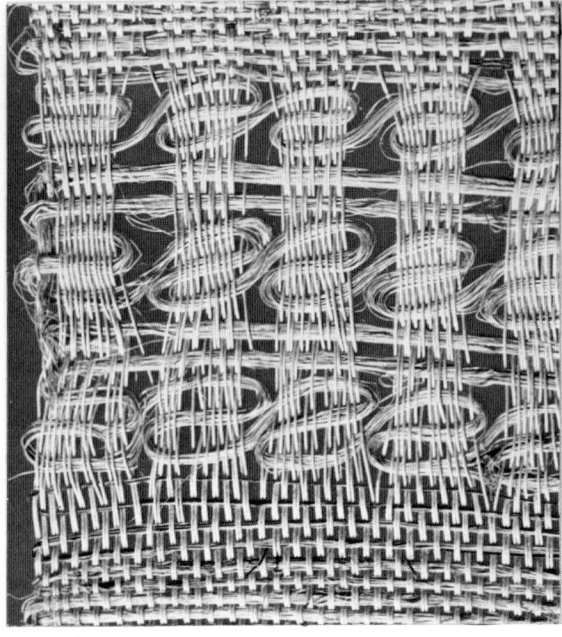

Treadle the next tabby and weave 4 rows with flax.

Now work a diagonal medallion in a contrasting thread (in this case unspun sisal was used), starting with 6 warp ends from the right-hand side, then 12 as before, thus making the hooking hole halfway across the original medallion.

N.B. Working small medallions on fine weaving more than 4 rows of tabby may be necessary. The pulling of the pattern thread taut or otherwise influences the shape of the medallion from circles to ovals, from squares to rectangles—so, also, does the thickness of the threads control the shape.

DANISH MEDALLION

DANISH MEDALLION. This open weave is excellent because of its range of variations in design. It can be worked straight up and down the warp, or across to make a border, or diagonally, or in blocks. The medallions can vary in shape and size in the same piece of weaving.

Directions for the sample shown in the photograph:

Weave 2 rows of tabby in a contrasting colour (orange jute).

Weave 4 rows of tabby with flax.

On the next tabby row start the medallion. Decide the size of it and calculate the threads in the warp. (In this case 12 warp ends were used.)

Treadle tabby and leave the shed open. Pass the coloured jute through 12 ends.

At this point insert a crochet hook down between the 2 original tabby rows woven in colour jute and reach up behind the 4 flax rows to hook the new jute thread. Bring a loop of it out where the crochet hook was inserted and thread the jute thread through the loop and on through the next 12 warp ends. Continue forming medallions across the warp to the left edge.

Danish Medallion worked in sisal, natural, and dyed sisal fibres.

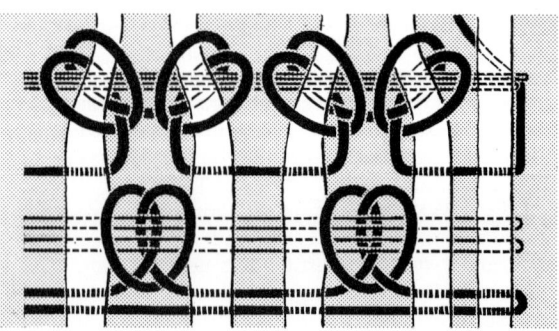

NEEDLE WEAVING ON THE LOOM

This type of openwork is made with the fingers or embroidery needle, wrapping threads around groups of warp ends. Groupings can be in blocks of equal sizes of similar threads, or elongated with even or uneven open areas, or geometric patterns of different colour blocks.

Directions for the sample shown in the photograph:

Work on a *closed* shed.

Select thick threads—calculate the number of blocks for the width of the warp—have as many "butterflies" or small balls of thread as there are blocks or sections. In this case 18 warp threads formed a block, 3 groups of 6 warp ends.

For the 1st block: wind thread in and out the 3 groups 10 times.

For the 2nd block: re-arrange the 3 groups of 6 warp ends and wind as before 10 times.

For the 3rd and 4th blocks: change to the unspun flax for contrasting texture.

For the 5th and 6th blocks: repeat 1 and 2.

To make a "butterfly": between your thumb and your little finger of the same hand wind a series of figure-eights. Wrap thread several times to secure in the middle. The beginning loose thread should pull out easily. These "butterflies" are quickly made and replace small shuttles in tapestry weaving, besides being inexpensive and easy to manipulate when working with a number of different-coloured threads.

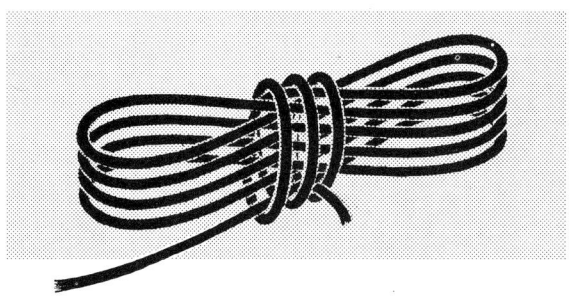

An example of the "Butterfly".

An example of needle weaving grouped in three's.

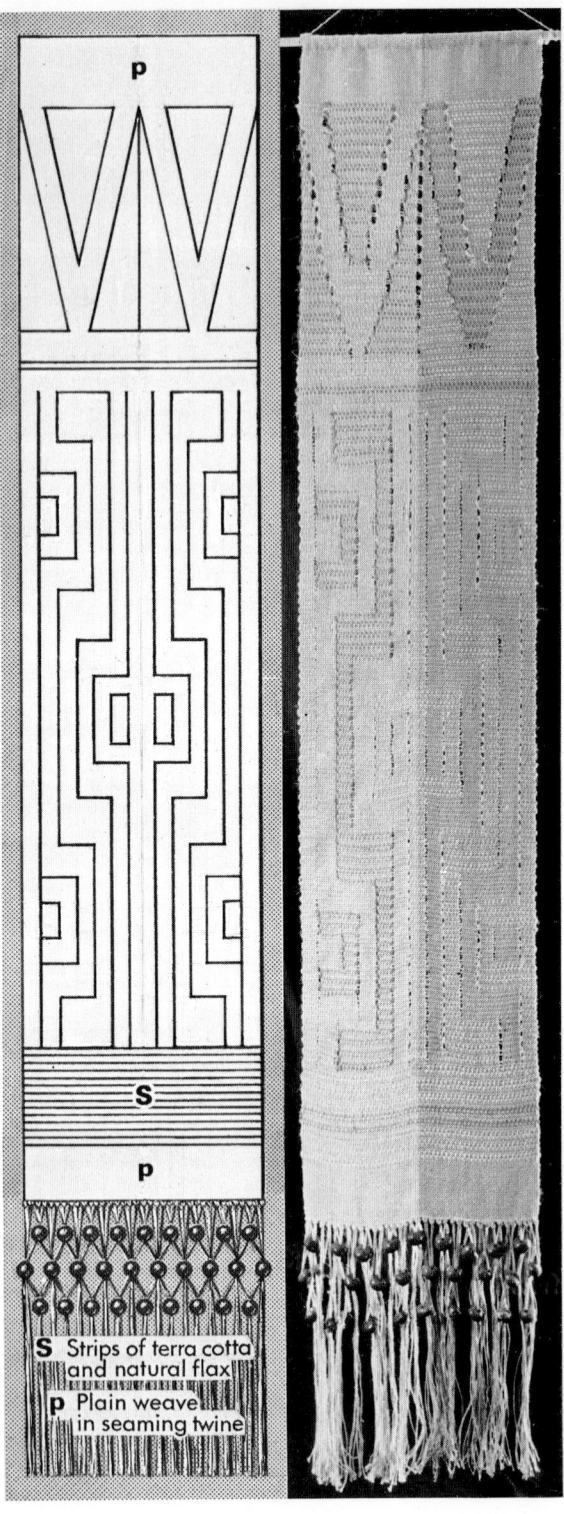

The finished panel with the tapestry samples sewn in place on the warp ends. For the tassel the warp ends were divided into 4 sections for the last 6 in.

Traditional Maori rafter patterns are adapted to weave this flax hanging.
Threading directions on page 49.

S Strips of terra cotta and natural flax
p Plain weave in seaming twine

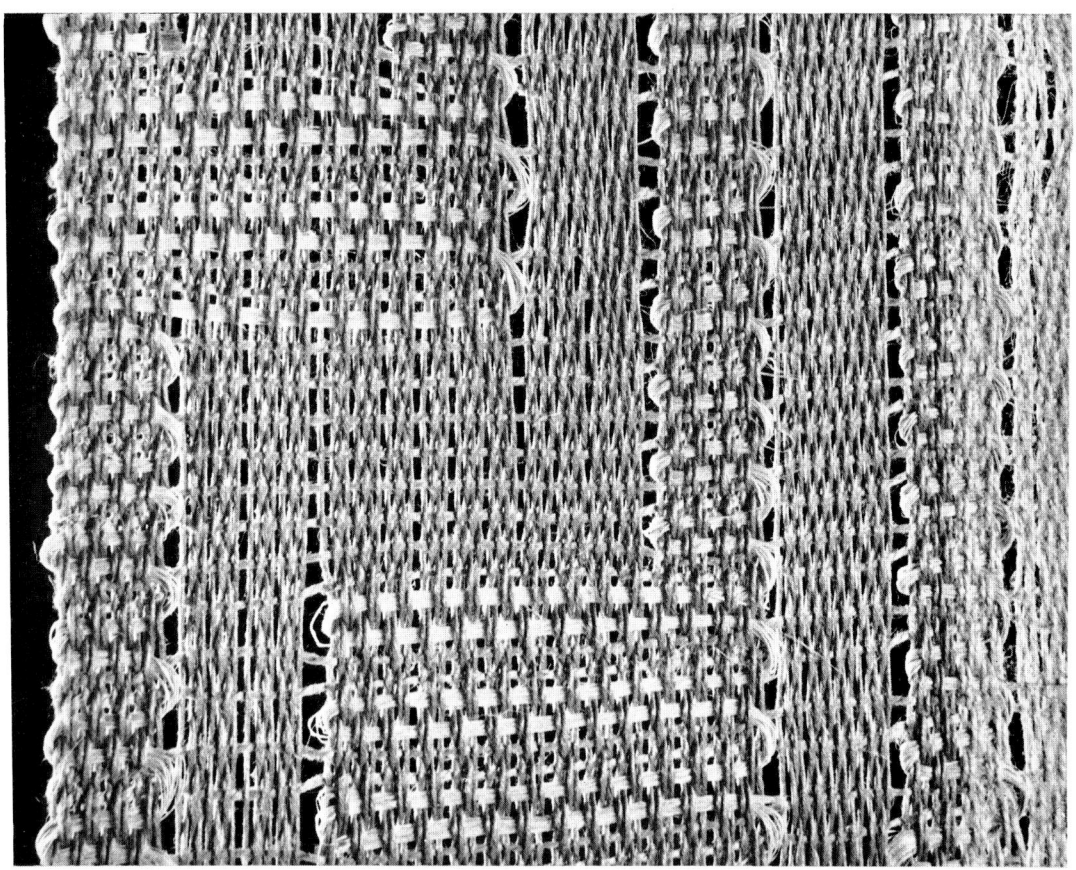

Details to show the treadling of shafts 1 and 2, 3 and 4, when the flax was
introduced: 1 and 3, 2 and 4, shafts when the flax seaming twine was treadled.

A PANEL OF WEAVING AND STITCHERY

4-shaft table loom or 2-shaft loom.

WARP: Hayes linen No. 18, 3 Cord (or its
equivalent).

WEFT: Threshed flax and hemp.

WARP ENDS: 80.

ENDS PER INCH: 16.

REED: No. 8.

WIDTH IN REED: 5 in.

DENTING: 2 per dent.

THREADING: Tabby, i.e. 4, 3, 2, 1 for 4-shaft,
2 + 1 for 2-shafts.

TREADLING: Levers 1 + 3 } for the flax and hemp
Levers 2 + 4 } separating the tapes-
try samples.
Levers 1 + 2 } for the side borders
Levers 3 + 4 } using flax only.

N.B. This panel frame may be used in a variety of
ways. For example, the tapestry insets which are sewn
in on the loom may be replaced with Maori taaniko
weaving samples, or wool stitchery emblems, or with
dried plant forms, seeds, etc., combined with stitchery.

WEAVE A WALL HANGING WITH FLAX INTRODUCING MAORI DESIGNS

WARP: Flax seaming twine 2-ply twist Stewart's
linen lockstitch size 2, a 7-cord in terra cotta
colouring.

WEFT: Threshed flax natural colour, threshed flax
dyed terra cotta.

WARP ENDS: 110 of flax seaming twine, 110 of
Stewarts linen lockstitch.

ENDS TO THE INCH: 16.

REED: 8.

DENTING: 2 per dent.

THREADING: Tabby.

TREADLING: Table loom 4-shaft—
1 and 2 } when inserting the flax.
3 and 4 }
1 and 3 } i.e. 2 rows of tabby in
2 and 4 } flax seaming twine.
Repeat this sequence throughout.

FINISHED WIDTH: 13½ in.

FINISHED LENGTH: 77 in., which includes a 14 in.
fringe weighted down with 21 ceramic beads.

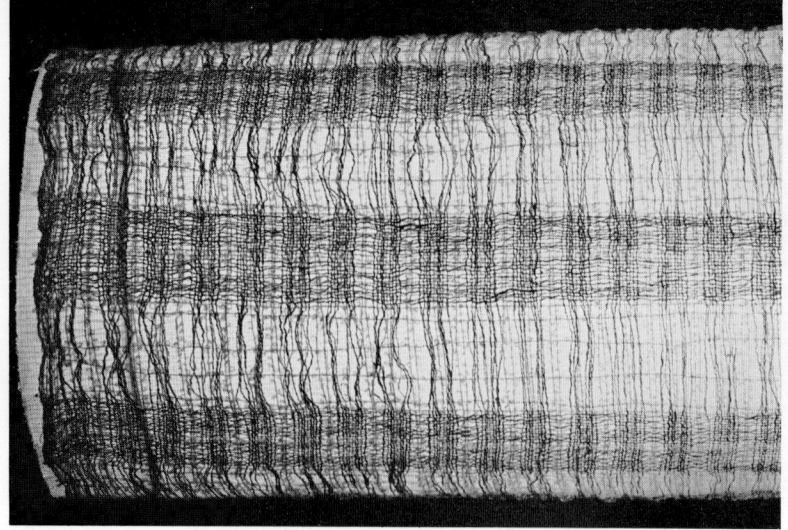

The lampshade woven material ready to be made up. This is a spaced warp and weft woven in novelty yarns.

LAMPSHADE

WARP: Natural tow yarn, novelty yarn.
WEFT: Same as warp.
WARP ENDS: 277 for 20 in. width.
REED: 10.

THREADING:

Tow yarn.	4	4		4		4		4	= 277
novelty yarn.			1		2		1		threads

24 Times

DENTING: Tow yarn 2 threads to a dent 2 times. Novelty yarn 1 thread to a dent 1 time. Tow yarn 2 threads to a dent 1 time. Skip 2 dents. Novelty yarn 2 threads to a dent 1 time. Skip 2 dents, repeat.

TREADLING: (a) Tabby weaving 1 and 3, 2 and 4 for 2 in.
(b) Place an inch-wide stick in the shed.
(c) 2 shots of tabby.
(d) Place 2nd stick in shed.

Repeat all for desired length.

The sticks keep the spacing even—remove them after each 2 in. of tabby and use them again.

REQUIREMENTS: A stiff buckram or white parchment or glass cloth the size of the weaving.
A good PVA glue.
Glue the weaving with the PVA on to the stiff background, keeping the open-work lines in the woven cloth very straight.
Make up lampshade as desired.

CIRCULAR FLAX MATS IN PLAIN WEAVE

WARP: Handspun flax.
WEFT: Handspun flax.
WARP ENDS: 145 for a 14 in. finished circle width.

ENDS PER INCH: 10.
REED: 10 (N.B. use 8 dent for thickly spun flax).
DENTING: 1 per dent.
THREADING: Tabby.
TREADLING: 1, 2 on foot loom, table looms 1 and 3.
2 and 4.

When off the loom draw accurately the size of cir le required and with the zigzag or overlocking stitch on the sewing machine finish the edge to prevent fraying.

N.B. On this threading weave any type of bag—a variety of handles can be woven in flax on the inkle loom (see *Spin Your Own Wool*, page 32).

A BEACH HAT FROM *PHORMIUM TENAX*

To Make the Circular Frame: Take a length of ½ in. cane approximately 52 in. long. Soak it in water and when still damp bend it to make a circle (diameter 15½ in.). Taper the joined edges, nail with the finest ½ in. nail and bind with string over the join for 3 in. Gently tack fine nails around the outer circumference, spacing ½ in. apart.

Materials required to Make the Hat:
Circular frame.
Threshed flax of a rough texture.
Flax twine.
Stiffening for the brim, preferably, prepared raw flax, or kiekie or pingao.

Referring to the casting-on technique for taaniko weaving (see the *Art of Taaniko Weaving* by S. M. Mead, pages 76–78) and using the flax twine, cast on

50

100 strands of threshed flax, the strands being ⅛ in. – ¼ in. in thickness. This number should correspond to the number of nails around the circumference of the frame. On the strands leave a good 6 in. to trim later for a fringe and 14 in. to weave the hat. There will be 100 loops which now can be slipped over the nails on the circular frame. To prevent them slipping off it may be necessary to run a piece of masking tape around the circumference.

Weave 3 or 4 rows 2½ in. – 3 in. apart, making the length of them shorter towards the crown so that the hat becomes a pyramid shape. A wide leno twist in one spacing is effective. Bind carefully before cutting off the excess strands of flax and turn the hat inside out. Use the binded flax ends to spread out to form a flat crown. Finish the outside with a plait of flax if desired.

To give the beach hat a necessary stiffness and shape there are several alternatives to use in the weft materials after the loops have been slipped on to the circular frame. Kiekie, which is a climbing vine much lighter in colour than flax, stiffer to feel, and shorter in fibre, was used by the Maori for their tukutuku panels and is one of the best alternatives. It resembles raffia. Also pingao, a sand grass grown near the New Zealand coastline and quite yellow in colour, blends exceedingly well with the *Phormium tenax*. These natural materials, like freshly-cut flax, need to be softened while still moist after cutting. To do this split the flax into approximately ½ in. strands (kiekie and pingao are already this narrow width) and with the back of a blunt knife or a shell put the strands over the knife edge to soften them as if you were pulling a satin ribbon between your thumb and first finger. Then these natural fibres can be easily twisted, plaited or rolled as desired—soaked in water for several days awaiting use—the flax boiled to bleach—stretched and rolled when drying depending on the effect required and the necessary stiffness.

Right: The Jamaican hat turned inside out to show the rows of weaving.

Below: The flax loops slipped onto a section of the circular frame.

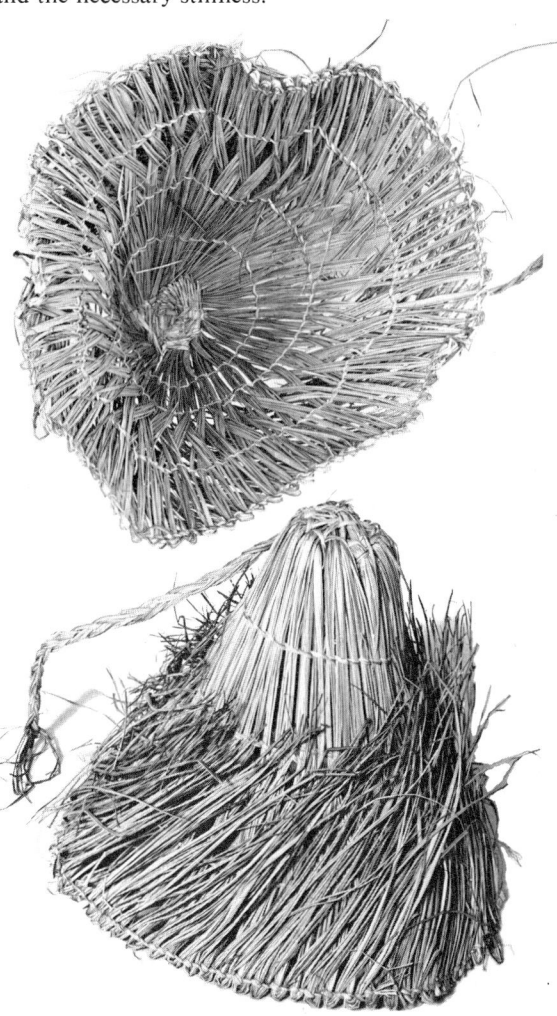

The hat made in *Phormium tenax* before being turned inside out.

The Jamaican hat when finished. It is woven on a circular frame and can be folded without damage.

Chapter 6

COLOUR IN OUR WOOL

ALTHOUGH there is certain charm always about natural colouring in wool and the subtle blends of plant-dyed colours with the natural, there is also a place for the chemical dyes that modern scientists have perfected to such a high standard. Colour is part of our modern society—it is today's fashion—and for spinning and weaving to flourish and look vitally alive it must go with the times. Just as an artist's painting can be highlighted with a splash of vibrant colour in the right place, so woven fabrics need this aliveness.

A weaver must be very conscious of colour—it is just as vital as the structure of the threads and the knowhow of using them. Fortunately there are many sources from which to learn about colour. Nature itself is the best of all teachers, and by far the most exciting. Take a flower, a leaf, a stone, a shell, the bark of a tree, a bird's feather, a cut fruit or vegetable —just any natural object that appeals to you.

With a set of coloured pencils or pastels reproduce on paper all the colours you can see in that object. Now on a ruler or strip of white cardboard wind coloured threads to match the colours in your sketch. Quite often the textural appearance of your natural object will suggest the type of weave construction, e.g. the delicate shading of the petal of a flower might require the honeysuckle weave, or one of the diamond weaves, whereas a crinkly lettuce or cabbage leaf would suggest an all-over twill variation.

Having wound these coloured threads touching side by side and not overlapping, count how many threads equal 1 in. on a ruler, remembering to leave space for your weft yarns to pass up and out between them. Thus the coloured threads cannot be pushed too close together along the ruler. This will indicate how many warp ends to thread in each dent and which reed to use to make the same number of threads per inch. It is advisable to assemble a scrap book for colour references—coloured photographs, illustrations, wrapping papers designed in colour, dress material samples, colour charts from paint shops. Indeed, from the latter build an interesting colour wheel to show the inter-relationship of colours—their value and intensity.

HOW TO BUILD A COLOUR WHEEL

With a compass draw a circle and subdivide into 12 sections. Select the primary colours from a paint or dye chart—red, yellow, and blue—and cut the sections to size and paste them on the circle equally one-third apart.

Select the secondary colours—green, orange, and violet—and space them in the wheel as shown in diagram.

> Red and yellow make orange.
> Red and blue make violet.
> Blue and yellow make green.

This will leave 6 spaces on the wheel for the intermediate colours, which are produced by adding extra amounts of one of the primary colours to a secondary colour. The term for this is *hue*, and there can be basic or primary hues, secondary hues, and tertiary. Into these last 6 spaces it is far more interesting to paste very small narrow strips of the right shaded tonings; e.g. in the space between the primary blue and the secondary green, paste the intermediary blue-green shades showing those with the most blue nearest the blue section, while the greener shades start near the green space.

Black and white or dark and light of other colours added to any primary, secondary, and intermediate will give colour *tones* (light tones called *tints*—darker called *shades*). Colour *intensity* is the brilliance. Colour *value* is its quality and relation to black and white.

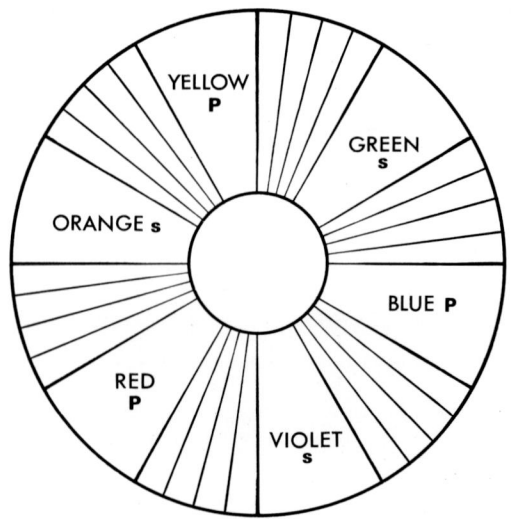

The six striped areas are for the intermediary colours.
P = primary colours.   S = secondary colours

HOW TO WEAVE A COLOURED SAMPLER

In a woven fabric where colour is used in the warp and crossed in and out with weft colours this intermingling of threads can be surprising and sometimes disappointing. Therefore, it is a wise precaution for every weaver to make as a beginning-project a colour sampler to keep always for reference. For the average home weaver one sampler of 1 in. – 1¼ in. squares in as many different colours as will extend across her loom will be adequate, but prolific weavers of material may prefer several samplers in the different colour combinations. Try first the 12 colours from the colour wheel, page 52. Weave the sample with the same colours in the same order as that in which they are threaded. There should be the same number of wefts per inch as warp colours per inch. For example, if you have calculated 1¼ in. of each colour of warp threads, make from a piece of cardboard or drawing paper a measuring-square of 1¼ in. Cut out a notch exactly 1¼ in. down. Use this test strip to measure the number of wefts to the 1¼ in. square. (It is much quicker than counting each row and is very accurate.)

It will be noted that where red crosses red, the resulting square will still be red but where red crosses yellow the square will be orange. Red crossing some of the green tonings will give a dull, muddy combination.

THE SETTING for a 30 colour woven sampler.
WARP: 30 colours of 1¼ in. each.
WEFT: Same as for warp.
WARP ENDS: 450.
ENDS PER INCH: 12.
REED: 12.
DENTING: 1.
WIDTH IN REED: 37½ in.
THREADING: Tabby.
TREADLING: Table looms 1 and 3, 2 and 4.

Of course the size and kind of yarn selected will have some overall influence on the tonings as well as the setting in the reed. Fine wool threads, set at 24 to the inch, will intermingle in warp and weft and show a more integrated coloration than a thick cotton set at 12 or 15 ends per inch.

SEEING COLOUR IN FLEECES

Quite often the craftsman will come across the interesting and unusual fleece that pleases in every way, but he will also probably have three or four of lesser coloration that could be made exciting by the addition of colours that are already in the fleece but require exposing. (See back cover for examples.)

This is how to make a heather mixture. As a starting point try the following:

(a) 4 oz brown fleece.
1 oz lichen dyed wool.
1 oz bright orange chemical-dyed wool.

(b) 4 oz dark grey fleece.
1 oz maroon.
1 oz light purple.
1 oz white fleece.
½ oz scarlet.
N.B. This mixture was plyed with a shocking-pink fine worsted.

(c) 4 oz light grey fleece.
1 oz blue chemical-dyed.
1 oz scarlet red.
1 oz light purple.

(d) 4 oz white fleece wool.
2½ oz emerald green.
1 oz really dark brown fleece wool.

Now very roughly tease one of the heather mixtures with your hands, shake on this a little neatsfoot oil, and spin, making a knub thread. If you find it difficult to spin you can use your carders to make rolags, but do not card the wool too well, otherwise you will lose the knub effect of the bright colours and they will merge too much with the fleece wool. Try cutting the coloured wool as short as 1 in. – 1½ in. The spun thread can either be used singly, or plyed with itself to make 2-ply, or plyed with a brightly-coloured wool to further accentuate a colour.

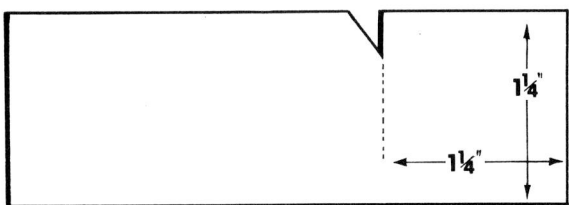

A 12-colour woven sampler.

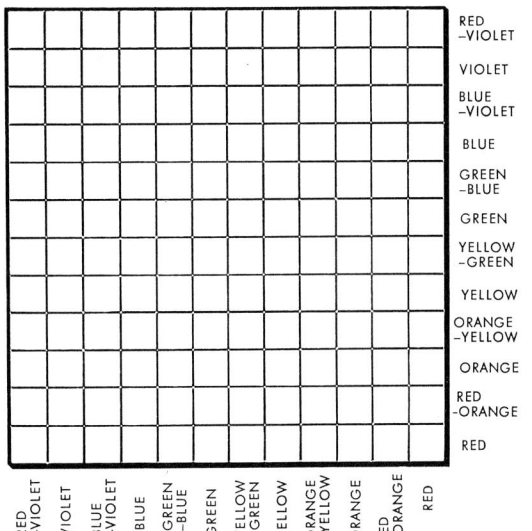

RED-VIOLET
VIOLET
BLUE-VIOLET
BLUE
GREEN-BLUE
GREEN
YELLOW-GREEN
YELLOW
ORANGE-YELLOW
ORANGE
RED-ORANGE
RED

TIE DYEING IN THE SKEIN ON A PREPARED WARP

Tie-dyeing is literally what the two words mean—tie and dye. The tying is done on yarn in a skein so tightly as to prevent dye from penetrating to the tied parts of the skein.

In weaving there are two ways to tie-dye—the tying of yarn in a skein, and the tying of yarn already wound into a warp. In the former method the weaving is uncontrolled; the colours may or may not weave into an organised colour pattern, but the shading effects can be very pleasing. In the latter case, controlled shading from dark to light is possible by dyeing either the beginning of the warp or the end of the warp and leaving a part of the warp out of the dye bath completely.

To Prepare the Skein to be Tie-Dyed

1. Stretch the skein firmly on either a niddy-noddy, or on a circular skeiner, or use the pegs on a warping board. Check the measurement (most skeins are 36 in.).
2. Calculate how many sections you wish to tie. For example

> 1 in. tie ...... 1 in. left for the dye.
> 3 in. tie ...... 3 in. left for the dye.
> 5 in. tie ...... 5 in. left for the dye.
> 5 in. tie ...... 5 in. left for the dye.
> 3 in. tie ...... 3 in. left for the dye.
> 1 in. tie ...... 1 in. left for the dye.

This makes a total of 36 in. With a very thick cotton, bind the skein as tightly as possible in the appropriate sections, packing the cotton turns close together and keeping the tension even. When you have completed the 1 in. (and/or 3 in. or 5 in.) bind back over the original cotton turns so that this makes a 2nd row on top of the first.

3. The skeins are now ready for the dye bath.
4. After dyeing rinse well and dry.
5. Now the cotton tie binding can be removed.
6. Rewind the skein before weaving.

By altering the length of the skein to correspond with the calculated width of the warp setting, and by planning the measurement of the tie sections carefully, it is possible to weave a geometric pattern.

Tie-dyeing can be a very complicated and skilful craft and is by no means confined to one-colour dyeing. It calls for much experimentation and careful calculation if you are able to repeat planned patterns.

If possible, keep parts of the skeins that are not needed to be dyed out of the dye batch completely by draping them over a stick balanced above the dye bath. This is easy to do when dyeing only the middle of a skein or the ends. This is an ancient craft specialised over many years in many different countries and, as it is creeping back into modern designing in varying forms, it is to these countries that the craftsman looks for knowledge and practical experience.

AN ORIGINAL WALL-HANGING WOVEN IN GOLD TONINGS

This wall-hanging shown in diagrammatic form in the photograph is planned as a balance of textured threads, woven shapes, and plant-dyed colours in gold shades.

WARP: Fine yellow linen used double for colour (Finlayson's No. 9 Patent).
WEFT: Yellow, gold, pale lemon, grey-green wools, yellow linen same as warp.
WARP ENDS: 280 of doubled thread.
ENDS TO THE INCH: 16.
REED: No. 8.
THREADS PER DENT: 2.
THREADING: Tabby.
TREADLING: Table loom 1 and 3, 2 and 4.
SKETCH PLAN OF DESIGN: Cut paper sections and colour them. Place these on sketch plan (16½ in. x 40 in.) to build up a pleasing balance of colour.

N.B. This is not a true tapestry technique because the warp threads were planned for colour to balance the colours of the weft. The homespun threads of plant-dyed colours were made to contrast with the smooth machine threads.

HOW TO MAKE A DIVIDED FRINGE. Fringe is always the most natural trimming and there are many ways of making it for edging in both needlework and weaving. Importance lies in selecting the "right" fringe to be a part of the overall construction. In this case, because of the finer warp set and the open character of the weave, a dainty edging was required to contrast with the heavier finish of the woven tapestry. A divided fringe seemed to suit.

To Make this Fringe: First make a line of small knots to lie very closely beside the last row of weaving—4 warp ends (i.e. 8 threads of Finlayson's No. 9 which are doubled for the warp) are sufficient to keep the knots neat and not too prominent. Make a loop, pull the 4 warp ends through this loop and tighten the knot only when it is in the position required. One inch below the line of small knots make the 1st row of the divided fringe. Three clusters of threads are knotted together for this.

> Second row: 1 in. below divide the bunches of threads that hang from the knots of the 1st row, take half a bunch from the right and half from the left and knot them together so that the knots come between those of the row above.
> Third row: Knots 1 in. down should lie immediately below knots of 1st row.
> Fourth row: Knots 1 in. down should lie immediately below knots of 2nd row.

In calculating the length of thread required for knotting, estimate twice the length of a finished fringe, i.e. a 6 in. fringe would need a 12 in. length of unwoven warp ends.

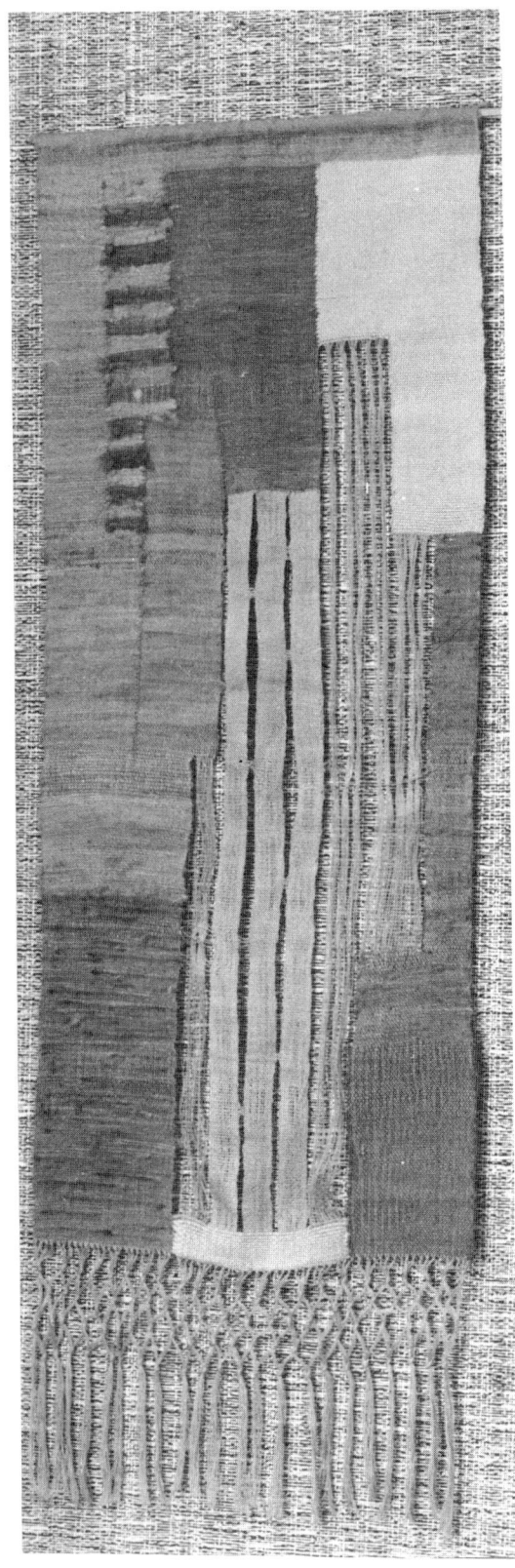

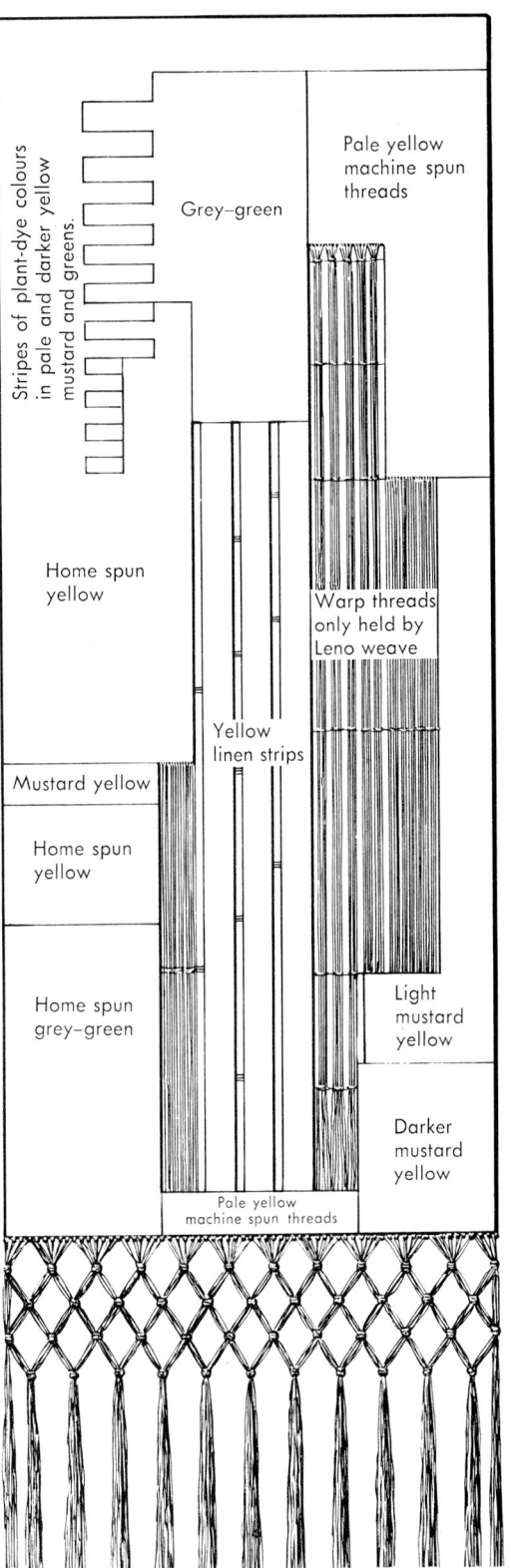

Stripes of plant-dye colours in pale and darker yellow mustard and greens.

Grey-green

Pale yellow machine spun threads

Home spun yellow

Yellow linen strips

Warp threads only held by Leno weave

Mustard yellow

Home spun yellow

Home spun grey-green

Light mustard yellow

Darker mustard yellow

Pale yellow machine spun threads

Experimental Embroidery: An example of Maltese tufting or tassel stitch worked with fleece wool on a brightly coloured background to give a raised effect. It is similar in appearance to the Scandanavian Rya knots in weaving and to the hook rug on canvas.

Chapter 7

EMBROIDERY WITH WOOL AND FLAX

WOOL and flax in their raw state as well as in the form of spun threads have unique characteristics necessary for modern stitchery. More and more embroidery enthusiasts either learn to spin their own threads or make friends with a spinner who will make the thread to order. For this reason I have included this section on stitches as a guide to further designing with wool and flax.

Embroidery is a technical skill like spinning and weaving, and has a long tradition of excellent workmanship handed down from generation to generation with variations in the actual stitches.

Why then is this ancient craft so popular today? The answer lies in that all-important word "design", whose styles change with each century. In our modern world stitchery has become exciting—needlewomen have discarded the commercial transfers and found the expression of their own ideas more satisfying, more challenging, and more compatible with modern artistic developments.

Through industrial advances the needlewoman has access to a wider range of threads and fabric materials —plain, textured, woven, printed, checked, striped, figured, etc.—all in fascinating colour combinations vital for appliqué. These were not available to the needlewomen of the Middle Ages. Progress, too, has given us the domestic sewing machine capable of simple and effective pattern stitches worked by machine quicker than by hand. This is another factor to swing the modern needlewoman to her own individual creations.

Basic stitches only will be presented as a starting point. The enthusiast will need to study further the many aspects of stitchery—appliqué, patchwork, quilting, tapestry known as canvas work, inlay, couching and inlay, embroidery, with beads, jewels, etc. Many and diverse are the books on these subjects and their study is a most rewarding one.

BASIC STITCHES. Because of the character of the wool and flax threads the sampler of basic stitches shown in the photograph was worked on dark hessian. It shows:

Running Stitch. This is one of the easiest and quickest to learn but it has great variety in thickness, length of stitch, and choice of thread. It makes a line of stitches with gaps in the fabric taking 1, 2, 3 or 4 threads at a time. Start from the right-hand side of your fabric and work your needle up and down running toward the left, making long runs, even ones, long and short, or crowded ones. Work with different colours, with machine-spun wool of varying thicknesses, fine and coarse handspun, textured threads of synthetics, wool straight from the sheep's back or threshed flax, coarse and stranded. Running stitch can be used to outline or to fill in colour. The photograph shows running stitch in fleece wool and in flax.

Single Threading on a Running Stitch. Make a running stitch as before. Take a contrasting colour and from the right bring a blunt needle just below the 1st running stitch and pass the thread under (not catching the fabric at all). Then loop the thread down under the 2nd running stitch, up and under the 3rd, down through the 4th, and so on.

Double Threaded Running. Do the single threading on a running stitch as described above, and reverse it coming from left to right, either with the same thread or a change of colour.

Back Stitch. Another simple stitch, but to be effective it must be very evenly worked. Bring the thread up from the underside of the material on the line to be followed. Take a small stitch back on the line, and bring the needle up in front at the same length as the 1st stitch. Take needle back to where the last stitch came out and continue to make these small back stitches along the line. It is a continuous line of stitches on the surface, showing a stem stitch at the back.

Seed Stitch. This is really a back stitch used in a scattered arrangement.

Stem Stitch. A useful stitch for stems and lines. Begin by bringing the thread up at the left-hand side of the line or the bottom of a stem, and work upward. Take a small straight stitch and bring needle up again at the beginning of the thread (see fig. 1) and continue to work along the line, with straight stitches of even length, always bringing the needle back and up at the end of the last stitch (see fig. 2). The wrong side should look like fine backstitch. Fig. 3 shows it being used as a filling stitch or an outline. Always keep your thread on the same side—you can use either side but don't switch back and forth.

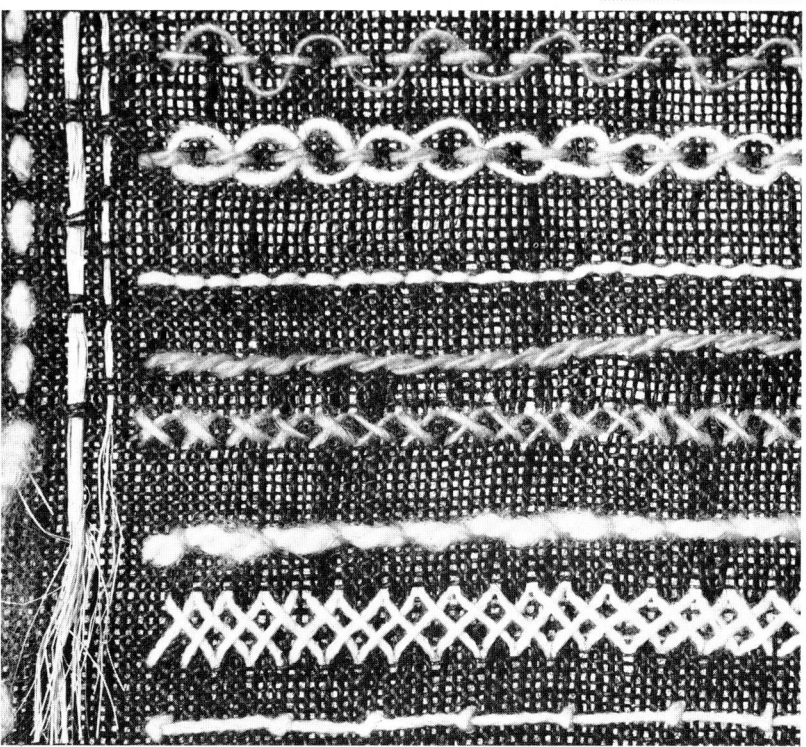

Single threading on a running stitch

Double threaded running

Back stitch

Stem stitch

Cross stitch

Couching

Herring bone stitch

Coral stitch

The following group, comprising the arrow or fly-stitch, the fern, feather, double-feather, cretan, and lazy-daisy with its variations, is used to work dainty areas for flowers, leaves, birds flying—or areas to be filled in lightly with colour.

Arrow or Fly. Thread comes up at A, loop it round to B, holding the thread firmly with the left thumb, insert the needle down at B and up at C. From C take a straight stitch over the held thread and down at D.

Cross Stitch. Though used frequently on canvas is a versatile stitch for any embroidery. Start at A, cross to B, under to C, cross to D, back to A. Work from left to right sideways or top to bottom lengthwise.

The under side of cross stitch should have lines either ‖ or =

If required the underside can show crosses also by taking diagonal-spaced threads from right to left, and come back crossing the threads at the reverse angle.

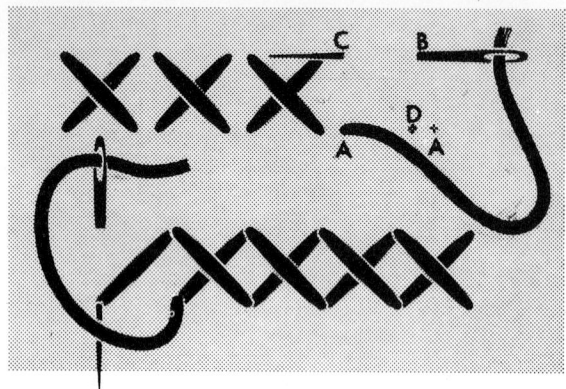

Feather Stitch. Bring the thread up from the underside of material on the line to be followed, bring thread to the right side, hold down with left thumb and take a slanting stitch back to the line. Take the next stitch on the left side, inserting the needle opposite the end of the last stitch and take a slanting stitch back to the line, each stitch coming a little lower than the previous stitch.

Double Feather Stitch. Two feather stitches to each side makes the double feather.

Lazy-daisy. A stitch often used to form flower petals. It is really stem stitch couched down. To make the petals of a flower bring the thread up from the underside of the material at the centre end of petal, hold the thread down with the left thumb and insert the

needle again where the thread came up. Bring needle up at outer end of petal, and over the thread being held down. This forms a loop. Draw thread up and make a small stitch over the top of loop, and carry needle down to next petal. Lazy-daisy can be reversed, the small stitch over the loop being lengthened and forming the centre of the flower.

Cretan is a wide version of feather stitch and lends itself to many variations. The description is the same but the needlewoman must make her variations.

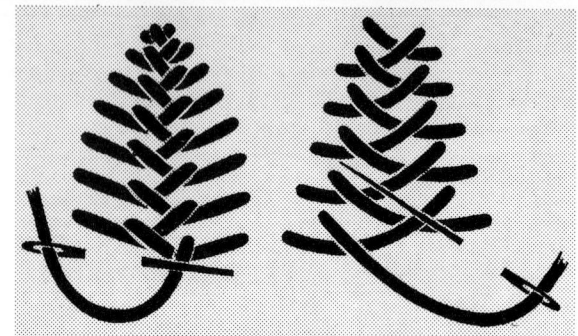

Chain Stitch has many variations. A single chain can be used for outlining or filling a background. Bring needle up from the underside, hold thread down and insert needle through the same place. Bring it up again in front of the loop as in diagram.

A double chain is formed by slanting the needle at an angle alternately from right to left and then from left to right.

For an open chain, insert the needle apart and not in the same place.

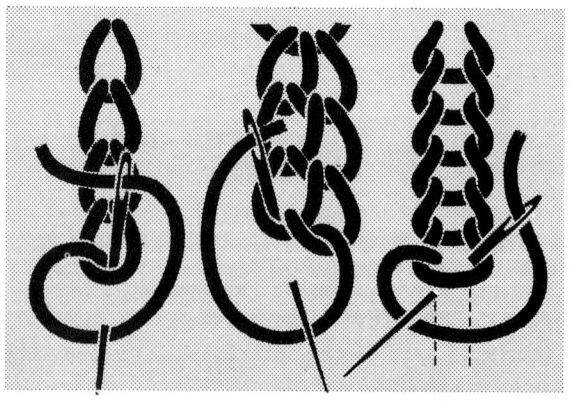

Couching. When a yarn is too thick to be sewn through

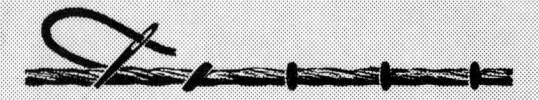

the fabric it can be couched. Pin the thick yarn in position and with another thread start at the right-hand side and over-sew with either straight or slanting stitches the thick yarn in position.

Herringbone Stitch can be used for couching also. Sew from left to right horizontally or from the bottom and vertically upward. Come up with the thread at A, cross to B, under to C, C to D. From D come back a little way to bring your thread up at E. Start the sequence again. Keep the threads parallel.

French Knots. A small stitch so useful in designing to accentuate the texture of a rough surface in contrast to a smooth—the knots give the chunky look. Bring thread up to right side of material and hold under left thumb. Twist thread round needle and insert needle into almost the same place, still holding thread under thumb until all thread is drawn through. In double French Knots the thread is twisted round the needle twice and the needle inserted and drawn through as in single french knots.

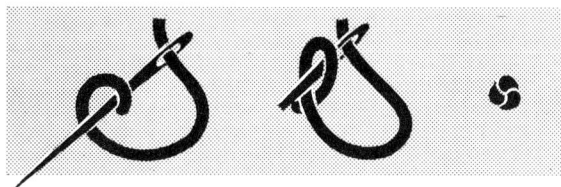

Bullion Stitch is like a long french knot and is used for making wheat, corn ears, barley, and small flowers.

Coral Stitch, as its name implies, is lumpy and can be described as a line broken with regular knots. The line can zigzag, curl, outline, etc. Work from right to left. Bring thread up at A. Hold thread straight to left with left thumb. Take a small stitch down at B immediately above the held thread. Come up at C immediately

below the held thread. Continue holding the thread until you have pulled up the knot.

Satin Stitch can be described as stitches lying side by side to make a solid area, but this is only one of its variations. It can outline in long and short stitches, sloping or straight. When filling in a solid area, first pad the design with a close running stitch, then work the satin stitch evenly and closely across the padding with the satin stitch worked the opposite way to the padding stitch.

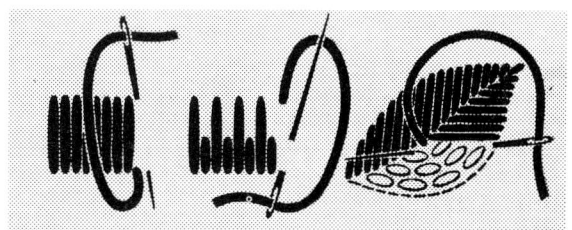

Blanket and Buttonhole Stitch. As the names imply, blanket is used for edging blankets and worked with a space between the stitches—buttonhole outlines button-slits with the stitches set close together to avoid fraying. Sewing machine attachments have replaced the handwork for the original purpose of which both these stitches were used. Nowadays they are worked in an imaginative way such as variable groupings, long and short stitches, double-sided buttonholing in two colours, couching with single and double holing.

Working from left to right hold the thread down with the left thumb, insert the needle at the top line and bring out again at the lower line and over the thread being held down. This forms a loop which when drawn up firmly, makes a purled edge.

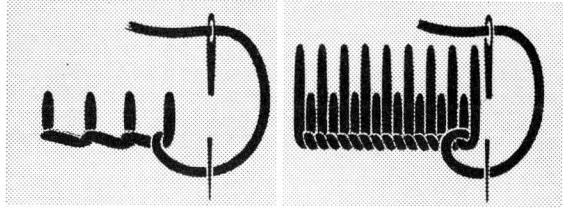

EXPERIMENTAL STITCHERY. Having learnt the basic stitches worked in the accepted way, now consider experimenting with them. There are hundreds of different combinations evolved by varying the many threads, their colour range, and the stitches themselves in all their shapes, sizes and arrangements.

Finished embroidery, like weaving, has to be planned carefully to suit the purpose for which it is intended, and this will influence, firstly, the choice of the fabric for the background; secondly, the character of the background will determine the selection of threads, their colour and texture—all making a harmonious blend. Some very bold stitches can be used only as decorative wall pictures, particularly if accent has been on a surface appearance that would not lend itself to hard wear and tear. But there is wide scope for creative work with stitches for practical use, and the following must not be overlooked: for wearing apparel, belts, braids, bags, clutch purses, cuffs, collars, cushions, aprons, toys; for Christmas decorations and amusing banners.

Keep a record of all your "stitchery" ideas in the form of a scrapbook. Include drawings from natural forms which have stimulated your ideas in colour, texture, and pattern; and make use of photography, not only to record your own finished work, as an artist does with his paintings, but also to photograph subject matter that will be of help in any later designing. Enlarged photographs can often reveal interesting complex pattern structures not easily seen with the naked eye.

The traditional needlework sampler should not be filed away for occasional reference. Incorporate it in some completed work that can be frequently before the eye. In the old days it often became a framed picture upon the wall, but it could just as well be an attractive pillow decoration for a bed, or a long doll, or a pillowcase animal with a zipped recess to hold night attire. Also, on a sampler of gairly-coloured stuffed stitchery birds, beetles or fish dangling in a mobile display, the flat and raised embroidery stitches catch the lights as they swing.

HOW TO USE THE FLAT STITCHES WITH WOOL AND FLAX

Running, seed, stem, cross, herringbone, satin and backstitches are all classified as flat surface stitches. The following diagrams are practical suggestions suitable for wool and flax threads. When handspun these threads give a rugged look in contrast to the smooth machine thread and, therefore, both can be used for effect and interest.

Coils of threshed flax couched in place or coils of 2-ply spun flax. Zigzaging worked in *back stitch* in single-ply spun flax thread.

Circular design in *running stitches*. Plant-dyed wool threads shade most attractively in this type of design.

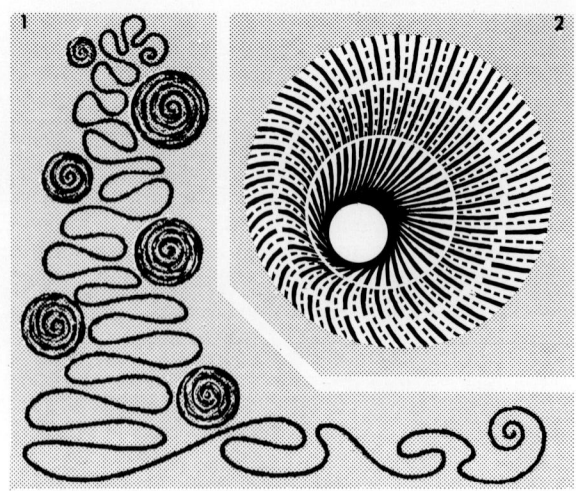

Herringbone in 4 different ways:

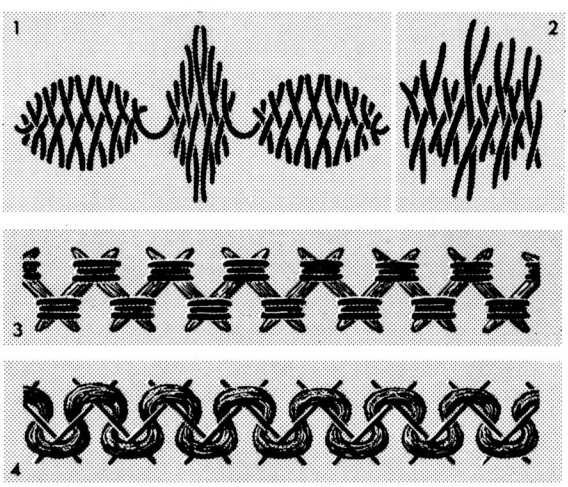

1. Irregular-sized stitches in wool thread of bright colours.
2. A squashed-up irregular look in handspun flax thread.
3. Herringbone tacked down with a contrasting colour.
4. Herringbone interlaced with a single running thread.

Some outline designs for either stem or back stitch:

1. Broken lines of coloured wool threads massed together so that no material shows through the lines.

2. A squared shape sometimes kept small to work in clusters—or large as an outline for different centres.

3. A curling design for fine wool thread or single strands of threshed flax.

4. Five circles of dyed fleece wool held in position with long flat stitches.

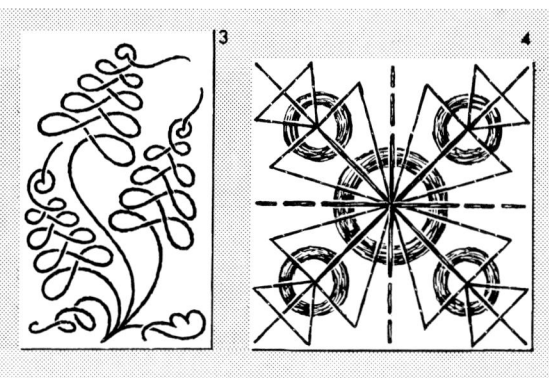

Satin stitch filling:

An oval design for either thick wool, or unspun flax, or both together, preferably an even thread. The stitch runs horizontally or vertically for effect. The dividing midline should be well defined.

Fly-stitch in couching. This looks effective in natural linen, or coloured linen, or coloured jute. Couching strips of either flax or sisal. Irregular groups of button-hole stitch can be worked in place of the fly-stitch.

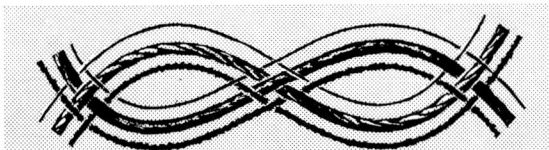

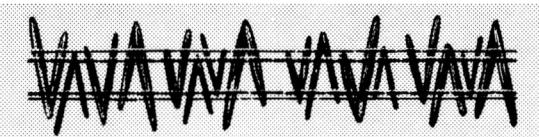

Threads of varying texture tacked down in waving lines. Use any threads of a knub handspun character and run the threads horizontally or vertically.

HOW TO USE THE LOOPED THREADS WITH WOOL AND FLAX

The chain, lazy-daisy, buttonhole, feather, cretan, all are grouped as looped stitches.

Chain over long running threads, very useful when the running threads form the feature of the design but need to be held in position at intervals only.

Chain binding threads secure in a different arrangement to form an outline.

A circle arrangement in long and short satin stitch with chain as decoration as well as spacing threads.

An open chain often required for couching thick threads.

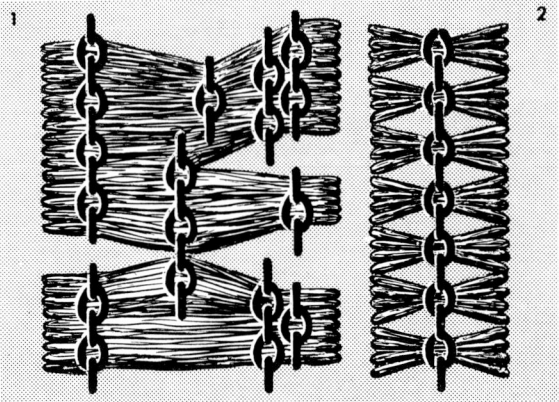

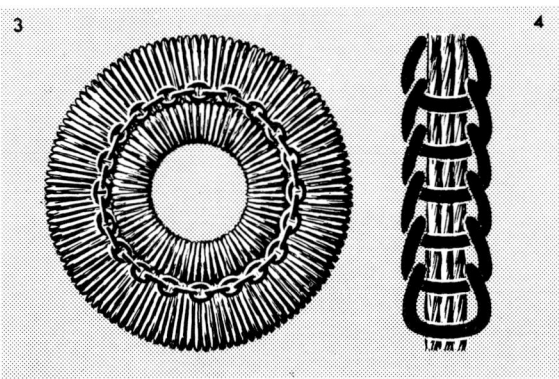

Index